The Art of Awareness

How Observation Can Transform Your Teaching

Deb Curtis and Margie Carter

Redleaf Press®
www.redleafpress.org
800-423-8309

Published by Redleaf Press
10 Yorkton Court
St. Paul, MN 55117
www.redleafpress.org

Printed in the United States of America

Excerpts on pages 1, 6, 23, 24, 44, 55, 57, and 92 are from *Learning by Heart: Teachings to Free the Creative Spirit* by Corita Kent and Jan Steward. Copyright © 1992 by Corita Kent and Jan Steward. Reprinted with permission of Jan Steward and the Corita Art Center, Los Angeles, CA; www.corita.org.

Library of Congress Cataloging-in-Publication Data
Curtis, Debbie.
    The art of awareness : how observation can transform your teaching /
  by Deb Curtis and Margie Carter.
      p. cm.
    Includes bibliographical references (p.) and index.
    ISBN 978-1-884834-84-4 (pbk.)
    1. Observation (Educational method) 2. Early childhood teachers.
  3. Early childhood education. I. Carter, Margie. II. Title.
  LB1027.28 .C87   2000
  372.1102—dc21
                                00-040290

Printed on acid-free paper

For Elizabeth Prescott, who first taught us the joy of observation. Her work has quietly shaped some of the best environments and practices in the early childhood profession.

Contents

Acknowledgments vii

Two Voices within a Teacher ix

Introduction xi

Chapter 1
A New Way of Being with Children: Overview of the Study Sessions 1

Chapter 2
Study Session: Learning to See.. 9

Chapter 3
Study Session: Observing for Children's Perspectives 23

Chapter 4
Study Session: Observing How Children Use Their Senses 33

Chapter 5
Study Session: Observing How Children Explore, Invent,
and Construct.. 43

Chapter 6
Study Session: Observing How Children Connect
with the Natural World... 55

Chapter 7
Study Session: Observing How Children Seek Power,
Drama, and Adventure 65

Chapter 8
Study Session: Observing Children's Eagerness toward
Representation and Literacy... 77

Chapter 9
Study Session: Observing How Children Form Relationships
and Negotiate Conflict 91

Chapter 10
Study Session: Observing Children with Their Families........................ 103

Chapter 11
Using Your Observations 117

Chapter 12
Getting Organized to Make Childhood Valued............................. 131

Chapter 13
Making Observations Visible 141
Sample Documentation Displays....................................... 157

Index 167

Acknowledgments

The ideas, experiences, and examples harvested for this book come from more places than we can remember or acknowledge. We apologize for any unintended omission of citations and extend our appreciation to all the instructors, authors, artists, and illustrators from whose work we have drawn inspiration.

A number of teachers and programs generously offered us their time, photographs, and observation stories for this book. Special thanks go to Rhonda Iten and the children and families of Burlington Little School. Rhonda's ability to see and tell the wonderful stories of children's activities has enriched our lives. Ann Pelo and Sarah Felstiner of Hilltop Children's Center continue to offer us terrific examples of how observation can inspire and transform one's teaching practice. Deadru Hilliard and Michael Koetje of Martin Luther King Home Day Care Center offered great patience and generosity in giving us examples of their work with children and their families. Thanks to Debbie Hoppy and Kara Bietz of the West Point Child Learning Center at Merck & Company; Wendy Jans of Puget Sound ESD Early Head Start at the Residential Parenting Program at the Washington Corrections Center for Women; Sandy Labyris of the YMCA at Lowell; Carmen Masso and Evette Ramos of La Escuelita Bilingual Preschool and Day Care; Joan Newcomb of the Little School of Bellevue; the ECE students of Whatcom and Edmonds Community College; and Jan Whitney, Cynthia Vatt, Valree Elarton, and Marilyn Crandall of the Mesa Public Schools in Mesa, AZ.

We appreciate the spirit of excitement and skill that Dilcia Yanez of the Mesa Public Schools brought to her Spanish translations for us. And we extend our continued thanks to Nancy Gerber, devoted family child care provider and photographer *par excellence*. Thanks to Kerry Ruef and the folks at the Private Eye who first introduced us to and generously supplied us with jeweler's loupes. And to Paul Fleishman who inspired us with his poems in two voices.

Our appreciation goes to Beth Wallace, Ronna Hammer, and Dan Verdick of Redleaf Press, who continue to strengthen the presentation of our writing.

And, as always, we are grateful to our families and friends, who once again endured our absence and preoccupation as we got swept into yet another book project. Their encouragement to pursue our passion for children and those who care for them makes it possible for us to do this work wholeheartedly.

Two Voices within a Teacher

I'm an early childhood teacher

I think of my work as

very demanding   very stimulating

It's as if I'm

An air traffic controller

trying to keep everyone on course
and prevent collisions

a bodyguard
teaching the children how to share
and get along with others

an architect,
designing an environment for discovery

a gardener,
tilling the soil, planting seeds for a love
of learning

The learning environment I create is clean and organized

I'm always buying new curriculum materials
and learning games

I arrange things with discovery and beauty
in mind, choosing things from nature
and loose parts for play in the classroom

If I could just

get the children to sit still and listen   take time to sit and listen to them

I could

teach them what they need to be ready
for school

discover their questions and encourage their
curiosity so they'll be excited about learning

I'm worried

they don't learn enough when they just play   they don't get enough time to play

There's so little time

to get everything I've planned done

to experience the wonder of childhood

Children need to be challenged to pay close attention and follow directions

Children must have time to race down the hill, splash through that puddle, sit under a tree, and gaze at the clouds

Watching children play

doesn't make me look like a real teacher

is the part of my job I love most
Children do and say the most remarkable things

It's true, children sometimes surprise me with what they know

I'm amazed by their insights and abilities

I know it's important to observe

Each child has to be assessed for their progress

Each child has so much to teach me
Watching closely I see so much growth unfolding

I so want

the parents to see me as a legitimate teacher

the parents to delight with me in what their children are doing

I have so much I want to cover with my curriculum

So much of my curriculum comes from my observations

When I let the children have free play

I have to have eyes in the back of my head to keep them safe and out of mischief

I see how they benefit from taking risks, and how inventive and capable they really are

This work

has so many pressures and demands

is sooo rewarding!

I'm thinking

about looking for another job

this job is one I want to keep for as long as possible

Introduction

If you're an early childhood teacher, no doubt your head is full of tugging voices and questions: What are the children really learning as they play? How should I handle all this pressure for school readiness? What will reassure parents that I'm a competent teacher? How long can I really stay in this job?

Competing interests in young children's futures storm around and within us. Early childhood teachers feel so much pressure to shape children into what society expects of them. In quieter moments we long to be with children in a different way. Then the prevailing tide rushes in with the language of standards, outcomes, and accountability. The wonder of childhood is pulled under and washed away once more, and with it, our love of teaching.

Waiting for you in the eye of this storm is the art of awareness and the joy of paying close attention to children. With close observation you can refocus, see the value of childhood, and remember why you wanted to be a teacher. You can learn to integrate the concerns of these contesting voices and a full measure of delight can return to your work with children. If observation is already part of your teaching practice, you may find an expanded focus here. If it isn't at the center of your practice, developing the art of awareness may transform your teaching.

Refocusing Our Work

The early childhood profession faces a critical juncture. We have come of age as a full-fledged profession with a core body of knowledge, code of ethics, professional standards, accreditation system, credentials, literature, and conferences. These developments are all wonderful, but for practicing teachers they often translate into giving more attention to checklists and paperwork systems than to the actual children, reflecting the overall trend in U.S. culture of overlooking the insights children offer.

In the United States there is no clear vision for the value of children or the role of childhood in our collective lives. We are willing to entertain children, make products for them to consume, and prepare children for adulthood, but we don't earnestly give them much attention for who they are right now. Except for brief moments of crisis, holidays, or campaigning for elections, rarely do the lives of children get public attention, nor do we hear people discussing how they enrich our humanity and our overall culture. Even parents and teachers fail to notice what children notice or let them lead us to new awareness and appreciation for their time of life.

Professor and author David Elkind reminds us that in the last fifty years our country has become more and more adult oriented, with children increasingly viewed as a nuisance. Shopping malls, casinos, health clubs, and the Internet have all been conspicuously developed as places for adults to gather. Parks, neighborhoods, and schools have been neglected. Most early childhood and school-age programs are isolated from the rest of the world, contributing to this generational apartheid in our communities. Strange as it seems, early childhood workplaces have grown to mirror, rather than transform, the invisibility of children in our society at large.

We are engulfed in a world of freeways, fast food, and electronic media. Commercialism has taken over the fabric of our lives, transforming our experience of play into the consumption of entertainment products, spinning our holidays into a frenzy of competitive shopping, and impacting our sense of ourselves as always needing to have and be something we are not. It becomes harder and harder for adults to remember who we want to be and what brings us deep pleasure or a sense of meaningful purpose in our lives.

The early childhood field itself is a clear target of commercial interests, even as we are marginalized and devalued in the overall allocation of resources and public attention. We, too, often behave as if we've lost our way, following the latest trend, rather than steadily cultivating a vision for ourselves. In our professional meetings and conferences, we are persuaded to spend our time rushing rather than relating, and consuming rather than creating. Our professional development and gatherings rarely focus on children's words, feelings, experiences, or thought processess.

Taking Up the Invitation

Children can awaken in us an understanding of what it means to be inventive, engaged, delighted, and determined to rearrange the world. If we listen to and watch them closely, they will teach us to be more observant, inquisitive, and responsive in our work and overall lives. It isn't easy to pay attention to children in this way. So much conspires to take us in other directions, even in the early childhood profession. The daily crush of tasks and pleas for attention is enormous. Our requirements and paperwork systems, our schedules and meetings and learning goals, can easily push childhood out of the picture. Unlike children, we adults have so many pressing agendas that we often miss what is right under our noses. Children invite us to take a closer look. This book invites you to learn the art and skill of observation. Doing so has the potential to change your life, not just your teaching, for the better.

The late Anita Olds, an expert in designing spaces for early childhood, used to say of licensing requirements, "Children are miracles, not minimums!" They come to us full of wonder, eager to understand and be competent. Yet amid our good intentions to teach them, we adults easily begin to deplete children's innate wellspring of zest for learning. In *An American Childhood*, Annie Dillard puts it this way:

> *No child on earth was ever meant to be ordinary, and you can see it in them, and they know it too. But then, the times get to them, and they wear out their brains learning what folks expect, and spend their strength trying to rise over those same folks (Anne Dillard,* An American Childhood. *New York: Harper Collins, 1998).*

When we neglect to see who children really are, we deprive ourselves of deeper sources of delight. We miss the opportunity to witness the profound process of human development that is unfolding before our eyes. Becoming a careful observer of young children reminds us that what might seem ordinary at a superficial glance is actually quite extraordinary. A string of ordinary moments for a child has been compared by Elizabeth Prescott to beads on a necklace, each one unique, yet related to the others, combining to create an unfolding work of wonder.

To be sure, some children don't appear to us as wonderful as others. They are the real challenges to our vision, sometimes requiring a magnifying glass to help us see what is really there. Whatever the stress and difficulties of our work with particular children, taking the time for deeper glimpses into their play, work, and thinking makes our jobs ones of continual exploration, invention, and flexible thinking. If we can keep our focus, we will get through the rough and bumpy times, past our blind spots, to find some new perspectives on even the most difficult children. Developing the ability to notice details and adopt different perspectives is a goal of this book. Bringing liveliness and enthusiasm to your work life is another.

Listening, Observing, and Documenting Is a Pedagogy

If we begin to value who children are, not just what we want them to be, a shift happens in the way we think about learning and teaching. Our jobs become more engaging and fulfilling. We also begin to envision a larger purpose for our profession—making childhood visible and valued for the ways in which it can enrich our humanity and contribute to our collective identity. To bring this transformation about, we need a *pedagogy* (a way of thinking about learning and teaching) that mirrors *our* vision for children, not the existing one of the popular culture. We need to move away from commercially packaged activities and make the time to develop curriculum collaboratively with our coworkers, the children, and their families. We must focus our attention away from the clocks and checklists to see what is going on with the children themselves. Teachers who subscribe to a pedagogy of this nature come from a place of curiosity, believe in children's capabilities, and know that they are engaging in a process that is unfolding, not static.

The benefits of this approach are far ranging. Moving children into the center of our focus teaches us more about child development, the learning involved in self-chosen play, and the components of a curriculum shaped around childhood. Looking closely, we can see the influence of cultural patterns and learn more about ourselves, our preferences, our biases, and our blind spots. Discussing our observations with coworkers and the children's families helps us to see things from different perspectives, allowing each of us to transcend the limitations of our own points of view. We create a collective context for mutual respect and learning from each other.

Gathering observation notes and other forms of documentation and broadcasting them as stories of children's pursuits gives them more visibility, meaning, and respect. The learning process is enhanced for the children as well as the adults. College teacher and author George Forman puts it this way:

> *We know that making children's ideas visible is an important goal. It helps children convert an activity into a learning encounter. Therefore, if documentation helps children make their own feelings, patterns of behavior, theories, and rules more visible and explicit, then documentation could become the primary means of educating young children (On-line dialogue on Reggio discussion list, 1999).*

Where can we see this pedagogy in action? Many would point to the schools of Reggio Emilia in Italy and the schools they have inspired around the world, including in the United States. We can see the seeds of this approach in the teaching and writing of college instructors Elizabeth Jones, John Nimmo, and Gretchen Reynolds. Their books, referenced throughout the chapters of this book, are rich with descriptions of children's play and teachers negotiating their roles in it. Teachers can turn to their writing again and again for reminders and inspiration of how children's lives can be valued and our differing perspectives on them negotiated.

Several practicing early childhood teachers have also written books, giving us a firsthand, vivid picture of how this pedagogy has been developed in their classrooms. Ann Pelo is a preschool teacher-author working in a full-time child care program. Her teaching is featured in three videos, *Children at the Center, Setting Sail,* and *Thinking Big.* She describes her evolving pedagogy of listening, observing, and documenting in the book she co-authored with Fran Davidson, *That's Not Fair!*

> *When I first began the practice of taking notes about children's play and making recordings of children's conversations, I didn't really understand how to use all the documentation I gathered. I did it because I'd read about it being the Right Thing to Do. I'd carefully transcribe a recorded conversation among children, then go on with the plans I'd already made. I mostly thought of the notes and conversations as ways to capture on paper the sweet and appealing thinking of young children. I'd share my transcriptions with parents, inviting them to "listen in" on conversations that they would otherwise miss.*
>
> *As I grew into the practice of supporting emerging projects, I learned more about how to use the documentation that I collected. I noticed myself wishing to understand if my guesses about the children's interests were on target or way off base, knowing that it mattered deeply to the success of an emerging project. I began to turn to my carefully collected notes for guidance. When I studied my notes and transcriptions alone or with a co-teacher, I could see "underneath" the children's words to*

the themes and issues undergirding them. I noticed when ideas were repeated, or when a theme showed up over and over. I began to see through to the heart of children's play. And with that understanding, I could respond in meaningful ways, taking an active role in shaping an activism project. I could better sup-ply the classroom with props that would sustain children's play. I could plan trips or invite visitors to the classroom. I could ask provocative questions of the children. I could develop strategies for the children to represent their thinking. Listening to the chil-dren is my best guide for supporting emerging projects; the doc-umentation I collect while the children play and talk deepens my listening (That's Not Fair! A Teacher's Guide to Activism with Young Children. *St. Paul: Redleaf Press, 2000).*

First-grade teacher Karen Gallas has written three books charting her journey as a teacher who makes children's words, actions, and artistic expressions a focal point for her own development. In her book *The Languages of Learning,* Gallas describes her pedagogy of creating the classroom as a research community.

This process of data collection is ongoing. It becomes part of the life of the classroom and is absorbed into the interac-tions between teacher and students. Thus, over the course of a school year, I compile an enormous amount of information that helps me to reflect on the classroom and to answer my more difficult questions about teaching, learning, and the pro-cess of education.... As a teacher-researcher, I do not deter-mine beforehand the categories of information I am looking for, the nature of the data, or the questions to be asked. Data collection is not a process used only for assessing children's learning or evaluating curricula. The process of data collec-tion, as it has evolved, has become a central part of my class-room practice (Karen Gallas, The Languages of Learning. *New York: Teachers College Press, 1994).*

Perhaps Vivian Gussin Paley is the best-known classroom teacher and author, with at least ten books published. Her writing simultaneously makes visible the richness of children's perspectives and the thinking process of an evolving teacher. In describing how her approach to teaching evolved, Paley says that in her early days of teaching, she found herself having trouble remembering who each of her twenty-six to thirty kindergartners were. At night she would develop schemes to try to remember each of their names, all of which failed. It was only when she set herself the task of writing a few sentences about something each child did or said that she solved this problem and began to know each individual.

This strategy engaged Paley for a while, but as it became routine, she found herself getting bored. "Bored!" exclaimed a teacher listening to this story. "How could you possibly be bored with twenty-six to thirty children to tend to? You must have been frantically busy!"

"Of course, I was extremely busy," Paley replied, "But that's very different than being bored."

> *When I say I was bored I don't mean with the children, I mean with myself and my job. I didn't find myself very curious, emotionally or intellectually engaged [in] what was going on. And because I was basically too lazy to go out and look for another job, I decided I had better make this one more interesting. So I began to create little games for myself which forced me to watch more closely what was going on. I'd try doing something one way with the morning group and then a different way with the afternoon class and then asked myself what worked better. I experimented with questions about how the boys and girls might respond differently, about what other activities might be least interfered with by the loud noise of carpentry, and so on. And, of course, once I approached my work with this kind of inquiry, everything changed for me. I discovered the remarkable world of children's perspectives and the unending delight of trying to understand the meaning of their play and stories (Personal conversation with the author, October 1999).*

Becoming a Keen Observer

What will it take for our early childhood classrooms to be filled with teachers who view children and their work with this mindset? Ann Pelo, Karen Gallas, and Vivian Gussin Paley offer us valuable models for how teachers can develop themselves from closely watching the development of children. Each of them has developed a teaching practice based on their deep respect for children and curiosity about who they are. Their curriculum leads to the same learning outcomes aimed for in conventional lesson plans but they use an emergent planning process with more meaning and relevancy for the children.

Becoming a keen listener and observer is certainly the foundation of the art of awareness. If you consult a dictionary, you discover that the definition of the word *keen* includes "showing a quick and ardent responsiveness; enthusiastic, eager, delighting in the chase, intellectually alert, extremely sensitive in perception" (*Merriam-Webster's Collegiate Dictionary 10th Edition.* Springfield, MA: Merriam Webster, Inc., 1993).

But rather than fostering "a delight in the chase," most instruction on observation makes it a tedious, arduous process, hardly the experience that Pelo, Gallas, and Paley describe. As teachers face increasing requirements to use checklists and complete assessments, observing loses even more vitality. A profession that allows this to happen sacrifices one of the most joyful, engaging, and intellectually stimulating experiences readily available to teachers. Children, in turn, lose the possibility of having their play and ideas taken seriously. Their activities are less likely to be what Forman describes as "learning encounters."

When you see your primary role as a teacher as closely observing children and communicating what you see, you find yourself surrounded by learning encounters. Becoming a keen observer is a way to learn child development, to find curriculum ideas, and meet requirements for assessing outcomes. It's also a way to keep from burning out in a stressful job. *The Art of Awareness* offers you a series of activities to develop yourself toward that end.

Using This Book

This book begins with a series of study sessions designed to heighten your observation skills. These chapters differ from other texts on observing, because they are designed to help you learn to really see children, not for the purposes of analyzing or doing anything to or for them, but simply to value who they are and the experience of childhood. The study sessions offer you activities to help you replace what you hope to see, any labels or preconceptions you might have, with a simple appreciation of the descriptive details of what you are actually seeing. We all observe subjectively and with the filters of our own experiences and values.

The first three study sessions offer foundational ideas and practical strategies to heighten your self-awareness, because the more aware you become of influences on your ability to hear and see, the closer you get to objectivity. These sessions are followed by a series of chapters focusing your study on specific aspects of childhood. Again, you will be asked to let go of your adult agenda or teacher urge to *do* something with what you are seeing, replacing this with the goal of really seeing what's there. In the Buddhist tradition this is referred to as *mindfulness*.

With these study sessions under your belt, the remaining three chapters of this book will offer you ideas and strategies for using your observations, getting organized and developing a documentation system for yourself, and finally, making your observations visible to others.

Throughout all the chapters of the *Art of Awareness* are photographs and observation stories, often with transcriptions of children's conversations. These will be as valuable to you to study as the text itself. You will also find examples of teachers' self-reflections and communications with the children's families to give you a picture of how observations can be used.

At the end of each chapter you will find a list of resources for further study when time permits. These include authors who are artists and naturalists, as well as practicing teachers and college instructors. They offer opportunities to further your thinking, sharpen your skills, and nourish your spirit. Ultimately, these resources and the way of being with children promoted in *The Art of Awareness* should enhance your life far beyond your job.

Living in the details of the human spirit leads to more mindfulness, liveliness, and overall pleasure in our lives. If we take the time to notice, each child offers us a glimpse of something promising in the world. When we make what we value and notice more visible to ourselves and to others, it becomes a resource for change. We create an active vision for becoming individuals and a collective culture that holds children and childhood as sacred and worthy of our utmost attention.

A New Way of Being with Children: An Overview of the Study Sessions

It takes practice for us to recover our ability to see, or before that, the gift of wanting to see. For so many years we have been learning to judge and dismiss, "I know what that thing is, I've seen it a hundred times." And we've lost the complex realities, laws, and details that surround us. Try looking the way the child looks, as if always for the first time.

Corita Kent

Observation Inspires Good Teaching

As you read the following story about Rhonda's classroom, consider the role that observation plays in her teaching. How does her close attention to the children's knowledge and interests influence what happens in her classroom?

As Rhonda sets up the room for her day with children, she brings the notes and photos she's collected from the past few days. She's been intrigued with the children's recent interest in arranging and sorting the basket of buttons she's had on the table. Her notes and photos show how they have been grouping them by color, shape, and size. Some have even put them in order from light to dark shades, and others balanced them in piles from biggest to smallest.

Rhonda decides to add something new today to deepen the children's explorations. She creates an enticing activity, using a mirrored tray that has compartments for sorting a collection of beautiful shells that she places in a basket next to the tray. As she puts out the photos of the recent button activity and arranges a few of the shells by size and shape, she thinks to herself, "The children have been doing such amazing things with the buttons. These shells should add something new. I'm excited to see what they'll do." As the children arrive, indeed two of the button sorters, four year olds Karen and Leslie, are drawn to the beautiful shell display.

Initially the girls work side by side looking closely at the shells, turning them over and touching each one with intent and careful study. Karen notices the spiral-shaped shells and comments, "Look, this one is pointy." 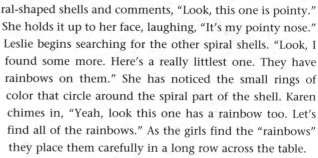 She holds it up to her face, laughing, "It's my pointy nose." Leslie begins searching for the other spiral shells. "Look, I found some more. Here's a really littlest one. They have rainbows on them." She has noticed the small rings of color that circle around the spiral part of the shell. Karen chimes in, "Yeah, look this one has a rainbow too. Let's find all of the rainbows." As the girls find the "rainbows" they place them carefully in a long row across the table.

Rhonda has been watching and now joins in. "You made a really long row of rainbow shells. The rainbows on the shells look a little like the rainbow pictures you make all of the time, the ones with all those colors." Karen's eyes light up with recognition. She eagerly gets a piece of paper and colored markers. "I'm going to make a rainbow picture." She begins to draw her familiar representation of a rainbow. After she finishes her colorful arched drawing she places the "rainbow" shells on the arch, fitting them from end to end. "Rainbows on rainbows!" she exclaims. This begins a new series of rainbow drawings that both girls cover with the "rainbow shells."

As they work Rhonda takes photographs and writes notes of these new discoveries and creations. Thinking to herself, she marvels, "These children have an amazing capacity to make connections. I never would have thought their classification work would connect to the rainbows they make all of the time. What a great moment; I'm so glad I noticed and offered my observation."

This small glimpse of Rhonda's work with children is rich with the elements of the teaching approach you will find in this book. Working with children in this way is quite different from focusing on the preplanned goals and objectives of most curriculum books. It also goes beyond traditional observation practices in early childhood settings, in which teachers collect data primarily for the purpose of assessment and measuring outcomes. While this is a valid use for observing, it is more limited than what we are suggesting in these pages. In fact, what you see in Rhonda is a teacher practicing mindfulness, flexible thinking, a willingness to take risks and work with an unknown outcome. She demonstrates the ability to move in and out of analysis and draw on a shared history with the children, even as she stays in the present moment with them. This ability helps her use their explorations as a source of planning, not to mention inspiration.

When approaching observation in this open-ended way, teachers must have a view of children as competent creators of their own understandings, deserving of the time and attention needed for experiences to unfold with deeper meaning. Teachers like Rhonda see the richness of these childhood moments and value children's perspectives and pursuits. Rather than spending time planning lessons and filling out developmental checklists, teachers with this approach spend their time observing children, working to uncover their point of view and understandings. They use their observations to guide their plans and actions. Notice how Rhonda does this:

- Rhonda arranges and rearranges the environment to ensure order and beauty.
- Rhonda provides open-ended materials for children to explore. She understands the kinds of materials that engage children—those with texture, beauty, complexity, and possibility.

- Rhonda observes closely and documents the details of the ordinary moments of children's explorations and actions. She uses her observations of children to help her expand on their thinking by providing new materials that invite them to pursue a line of investigation.
- Rhonda offers new perspectives, tools, and activities to support and challenge children's thinking. She makes suggestions and connects present activities to past interests, accomplishments, and experiences to help children go deeper in their work.
- Rhonda sees herself as a story collector and storyteller, gathering and sharing the unfolding events of their time together.

Why Study Sessions?

Because of the many demands and distractions for teachers, learning to pay close attention to children requires a commitment to systematic study and ongoing practice. This book offers you that opportunity. The study sessions were originally designed as a college course to counteract the experience of observing children as a cumbersome task. They offer you an organized system that will help you become aware of children in a new way. As you begin to practice observing, you will discover that developing the art of awareness is one of the most stimulating and nourishing things you can do for yourself and for children. It will make your job easier.

You will find that these study sessions are not designed as checklists to use or facts to learn. Rather, they offer new ideas, activities, and experiences to help you invent a different way of being with children. Each session will take you through a thoughtfully planned set of activities to help you slow down, become self-aware, pay attention, and think flexibly, critically, and in depth. Teachers who have participated in these sessions have found them useful for their work with children and in other parts of their lives. Here are some of their comments as they've undertaken the study sessions:

> Today I watched a toddler walk by my house holding his grandmother's hand. I watched from my window as he took tiny steps and stopped a number of times to step on a leaf, kick the grass, and point out some berries that had fallen on the ground. Since taking this class I now wonder what it's like to be entertained by stepping on leaves and grass and pointing to bright objects that I notice. I realize how much I pass by things and do not even notice them. I am quick to judge things that I've seen before. Now I have become more curious about things, and I am learning more and noticing more about the little things around me. It is so refreshing. —**Lindsey**

> I feel myself being stretched and growing. As I observe the children play now, I find myself examining their play in greater detail. I realize how I never really watched them before. I feel bad about it, but now I know so much more is going on than I thought. —**Judi**

> I feel challenged but also I'm really going through a learning process. I see now that observing is a process. The quotes have really made me think. The art of awareness activities allow me to visualize what I see differently and give me a different perspective. And the observation practice has helped me become really skilled at noticing details. I see the world around me so differently than I did a few months ago. I see it clearer and with more delight. It's a new beginning! —**Gail**

> This class has taught me a new way to observe, not only children but everything. It is different from anything I have ever taken. I never had to look at things before. I'm still trying to figure it out. It's hard sometimes, but I'm learning so much. —**Becky**

Components of the Study Sessions

The first two study sessions, chapters 2 and 3, provide foundational skills that will help you begin paying close attention to the children you work with. The next seven study sessions, chapters 4 through 10, are all organized similarly, and each focuses on observing a particular aspect of childhood. Finally, chapters 11 through 13 will help you communicate the story of your observations to other people in your program, including the children themselves.

Chapter 2, the first study session, is called "Learning to See." In it you will learn to examine how your own experiences influence your perceptions. There will be opportunities to practice noticing the difference between your interpretations and the details of what you are looking at.

Chapter 3 is called "Observing for the Child's Perspective" and offers strategies on how to shift from your teacher agenda toward finding children's points of view and the importance of their present life. This session will be the beginning of a number of activities calling you back to your own favorite childhood experiences to help you put yourself in children's shoes more easily. As you make the shift to seeing children's actions from their perspective, you will be reminded of how capable they really are. This view of children and the respect and trust it generates will transform your teaching.

The sessions in chapters 4 to 10 are all organized in the same way to help you practice skills and revisit the focus of each chapter through a variety of activities. The consistent methodology of the sessions will help you develop the left-brain skills of noticing the details of children's experiences and the right-brain awareness associated with an artist or naturalist. Detailed observation stories of children are included in each chapter, each highlighting the aspect of childhood focused on in that chapter.

As you go through each study session you will find the following components.

Quotes about Seeing

We walk around believing that what we see with our eyes is real, when, in truth, each of us constructs our own understandings of what we are seeing. —**Donald Hoffman**

In *Visual Literacy: How We Create What We See,* Donald Hoffman tells the story of a man who regained his sight after being blind since infancy. He describes the great difficulty this man had in making sense of anything he saw. Everything was unrecognizable and confusing, because he had no experience with the world of sight. He needed to shut his eyes to function because all of his understandings came through his other senses. This story is a powerful illustration of how we each see the world through our own experiences, bias, and filters. Having this awareness in our work with children helps us observe with more self-understanding and thoughtfulness.

As a reminder that we all see things differently, each of the study sessions begins with a quote and then a reflection like this one. These quotes come from artists, naturalists, poets, and others who spend time carefully reflecting on what they see. Use these quotes to spark, provoke, or challenge you to see how your own experiences may affect how you see the world, children, and yourself as a teacher. With each quote you will be asked to write about your reactions, thoughts, and the implications the quote has for your work with children. You are encouraged to share your responses and ideas with others. You also might want to continue to gather a collection of these quotes, post them, or keep them with you to help you stay alert to the limits of your own perspectives and to inspire you to see more.

Art of Awareness Activities

To give children and childhood the attention they deserve, we must bring a different mindset to our work. We need to "recover our ability to see, rather than judge and dismiss," as Corita Kent suggests in the quote that begins the chapter. The art of awareness activities in each study session will challenge your immediate responses and judgments and move you beyond first impressions and quick labels. Many of these activities are not directly related to children, but come instead from the work of artists, psychologists, and naturalists.

The learning activities offered here do not take the traditional approach to teacher education. They are intended to sharpen the overall awareness you bring to your work with children. Some of the activities will help you practice flexible thinking and shift your perspective. Others will ask you to tap your own creativity and express unique ideas. Don't be surprised if you find your head spinning or if you experience disequilibrium. Getting unsettled is part of the learning process that will make you a more aware teacher.

If you approach the art of awareness activities in earnest, they will help you reclaim your own sense of wonder and curiosity. Children approach the world with clear eyes and a refreshing perspective. They always raise their heads to marvel at an airplane when they hear its engines roar; they let ice cream linger on their tongue and drip down their chin; they stop to investigate the cracks in the sidewalk. Learning the art of awareness will help you approach the world as children do, with openness and the use of all of your senses. Your work will be the richer for it.

Remembering Your Childhood

Each study session is organized around a particular theme in the experience of childhood. These are themes teachers see every day in our work. To learn more about the significance of this childhood theme, you will be asked to recall the details and feelings of your own experiences. Your own experiences will set the stage for the observation stories that follow.

Observation Practice

Samples of observation stories are included in each session for you to study the details that hold the meaning and significance of the experience for the children. As you study the details in each story, you will learn how to collect and describe similar details as you observe. These stories offer you a snapshot of the ordinary moments of childhood. Consider them as invitations to be treasured and rich information to help you learn more about children.

Following each observation story you will be offered some questions to look closely at the details of the story to find the meaning and significance of them for the children. This will give you practice in looking deeper, beyond your own filters and teaching agendas. You can do this reflection on your own or with others.

After you've done your own thinking about the observation story, you'll find some additional considerations and questions to explore. We hope this will take your thinking further as you consider this observation in the larger context of childhood.

Take Another Look

After studying the observation stories, you are invited to apply the ideas in your own setting. These questions and activities will enhance your own practice and study about this particular aspect of childhood. You will find areas to examine, materials or activities to add to your environment, and suggestions for additional focused observations. As you continue to practice using these ideas and skills with children, they will become second nature to you. You will begin to readily value children's pursuits and become more creative in providing for them.

More Things to Do

Each study session comes to a close with ideas for more self-awareness and development activities. These will help you learn more about yourself, develop your awareness, and alter your attitudes toward children.

Recommended Resources

There is a list of relevant resources at the end of each study session, with short annotations for each resource. These books can help you study further the ideas from the sessions that spark your interest.

How to Use the Observation Study Sessions

The guidelines in each of the study sessions suggest ways you can work on your own, with a partner, or as part of a group. Whenever possible, find another person to work with. This collaborative study can be arranged in any number of settings, depending on your use of this book—in staff meetings, college classes, seminars, mentor programs, or informally among colleagues. Working with others will give you a variety of perspectives, more lively discussions, and more in-depth understandings of the usefulness of the activities in each session. You will always find more details, insights, and possibilities when there are more eyes, ears, and points of view focused on an observation.

The time frame for each session can be adjusted, depending upon your individual or group needs and schedule. The activities can easily take three or four hours, with additional time devoted to follow-up suggestions. You will need to find a system that works for you, one that helps you discipline yourself for the practice required.

Slow Down and Study

With this preview you are now ready to start your journey into *The Art of Awareness*. Give yourself time, practice mindfulness, and enjoy what you discover. At times you may find yourself in disequilibrium because your brain and body have been set in their ways for so long. Wherever you are in your own development, take this opportunity to expand the vision you have for yourself and the children in your life.

Learning to See

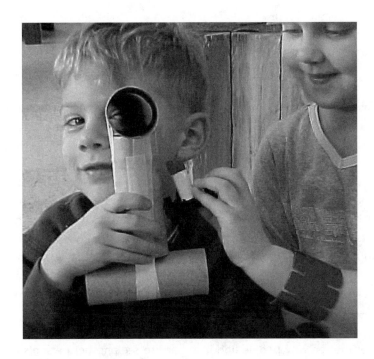

We do not really see through our eyes or hear through our ears, but through our beliefs. To put our beliefs on hold is to cease to exist as ourselves for a moment.

Lisa Delpit

Learning Goals for This Study Session

In this study session you will

- Reflect on your own mental filters and how they influence your perceptions
- Distinguish the difference between descriptions and interpretations
- Recognize the components of observation skills
- Practice seeing the details of an observation
- Explore flexible thinking with perception exercises

Reflect on the Quote

When learning to observe, we have to begin by examining our own experiences and perspectives. As you read the Lisa Delpit quote above think about these questions:

– What does it mean to you?
– What experiences does it remind you of?
– How do you think it relates to your work with children?

You can write about this on your own or discuss this with a partner or small group. You might want to use the responses below from other teachers to spark or extend your thinking.

> I think this quote means we all like to be right and in control, and that it is really hard to let go of our way of seeing and doing things. Sometimes my co-teacher and I really disagree about the different ways we handle children's conflicts. When we try to talk about it we are very defensive. I think we have to find a way to talk together with the understanding that we all have our own point of view and experience. We shouldn't start out thinking one of us is right and one is wrong. We need to find ways to have more open conversations. —**Jill, toddler teacher**

> It makes me see why people find it so hard to see another person's point of view. The quote implies we have to let go of not only our ideas but also our identity and who we are. I think people probably find that really scary. Wow! It means to me we have a lot of work to do to understand each other and ourselves. —**Dee, preschool teacher**

Art of Awareness Activity

Practice Exploring the Influences on Your Perceptions: Before we can observe children with a new set of eyes, we have to recognize our own filters, what influences the way we see things. This is the first step in developing the utmost sensitivity in our perception. The following activity will explore examples of these differences in perception. It requires that you work with at least one other person to compare your responses. A group of people will offer you a more lively discussion and more differences to reflect upon.

1. Find an interesting photo in a book or magazine that shows a group of people involved in an activity or interaction together or use one of the photos on the next page. Make enough copies for each person doing this activity together to have one.

2. If you are working in a pair, each person should look over the photo for a few minutes and, without talking or writing, make some mental notes about what

you see. Notice your emotional reactions to the photo as well as the details of what you see. Then, put the photo away, and take turns describing to each other what you saw in the photograph. Each person should describe what she saw without comments or discussion from the other person.

3. If you are working with a group, ask two or three people to volunteer to leave the room. (Volunteers should not be concerned that there will be tricks or judging of people.) Then, ask the volunteers to come back into the room one at a time. Each time, give the volunteer a copy of the photo to look over for a minute or two. Ask the volunteer to mentally note the details of what she sees as well as her emotional reactions to the picture. Take the picture away from the volunteer and ask for a verbal description of what she observed.

4. After everyone has shared their perceptions, discuss the differences between your observations. Use the following questions to guide the discussion.

– What were the differences in what each person noticed about the photo?
– Why do you think each of you reacted in this way?
– What from your background, experiences, or values may have influenced what you saw in the photo?

Understanding Influences on Perception

Each of us walks around in the world making meaning of what we see, hear, and experience. We have an amazing capacity to take in information and instantly make sense of it. In fact, when we can't make sense of something, we feel uncomfortable and out of balance. When we are in this state of disequilibrium, we work hard to find an explanation that gets us back to our normal, comfortable way of seeing the world.

From infancy we have learned how to make sense of what happens around us. We've discovered that facial expressions and body language give us reams of information about a situation. The tone of someone's voice creates a further impression. These are some of the strongest influences in how we see the world today. We instantly size up a situation without even realizing what factors are influencing us. And each of us does this in a different way, with the different filters of our childhood, temperament, and experiences.

If we become more aware of our interpretations, we can analyze the influences that come into play. Past experiences play a big part in how we make sense of things. Often we scan a scene to find what we recognize as familiar and then assign meaning from our past experiences. Our expectations about what we'll see also come into play. Consciously or not, we often see exactly what we expect to see. How we feel in the moment strongly influences what we see. If we are tired or cold or just had a fight with a friend, these experiences color our perceptions. And, as Lisa Delpit so clearly says above, our values and beliefs rush in as we interpret and judge a situation.

This photo activity offers a reminder of the differences we each bring in making sense of any given situation. Some people describe the concrete physical aspects of a scene, while others notice the relationships between the people and objects in the scene. Some people describe the details, while others describe the feelings they get from the photo.

The notion that we all see things differently is obvious. Yet, as we go about our lives, we usually assume that what we see is "true" and that others must be seeing the same things we do. When differing views are acknowledged, there is often conflict. We assume that if one of us is "right," then the other must be "wrong." Many of us are uncomfortable with conflict and try to avoid it. However, even if we are uncomfortable, we can recognize the opportunity to expand our thinking and our humanity that hearing different experiences and new points of view gives us.

This book challenges you to develop an active, conscious approach to seeing and interpreting your observations of children. The task at hand is to keep alert and self-reflective when looking at your own reactions to events and situations. Try to uncover the possible influences on your perceptions. Remind yourself that others are likely to have different, yet valid, points of view. Once you understand that you bring a set of mental filters to any observation, you can use this awareness to examine more carefully what you are seeing. The habit of immediately interpreting what we see limits our vision. We forget that what we are seeing is our own point of view, rather than something outside of ourselves. Changing this habit takes ongoing practice and self-reflection, because it is so easy to stay in our own "comfort zone."

Observation Practice

The following activities are designed to give you practice with the experience of seeing more intentionally. As you participate, try to let go of your interpretations and the pressures that cloud what you see. Don't think about writing or using the observations in any way. Strip away all of the noise inside your head about a right way to do this and allow yourself to be in the moment for what you can learn.

Practice Noticing Descriptions and Interpretations

One of the most difficult aspects of learning to observe is recognizing the difference between descriptions and interpretations. Here is an activity you can practice with different photos to develop your skills in separating descriptive data from interpretation.

Look at the following photos on your own, in a small group, or with a partner. Record all of your responses to the question: What do you see in these two photos? Be as specific as possible.

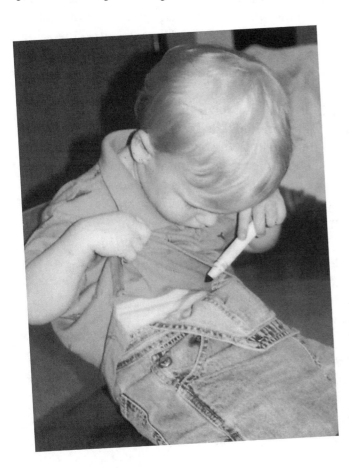 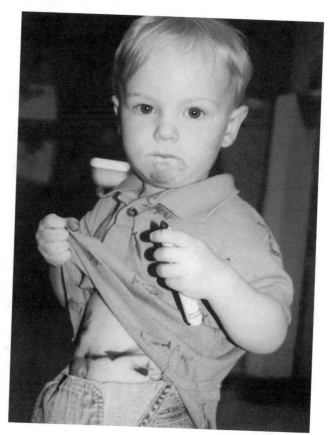

Practice Creating a Parking Lot

When we observe children, we often have initial responses based on our own mental filters and values. These can get in the way of really seeing children and the importance of what they are doing. It is helpful to acknowledge these first reactions and then set them aside in a "parking lot." You can write these on a separate page of your observation notes. A sample parking lot for a teacher watching Coe in the photos above might have notes like this:

– He's making a mess. I better stop him before he gets that black marker all over himself and his clothes.
– Yikes! What will his mom say if she sees I let him write all over himself? I can't let this happen!

Your first reactions may have merit, and safety issues may require you to jump in quickly to stop a situation. But unless there is immediate danger, it is important to notice those first reactions and wait before you intervene. When you watch closely, momentarily letting go of your first reactions, you can be more thoughtful about whether to intervene, and if so, how.

Looking over your observation notes from the photos above, decide if anything should be moved to a parking lot away from your descriptive observation data.

Examine your notes again and compare them to the list below. Notice that the notes are listed in two columns: one labeled "descriptions" and the other "interpretations." When learning to write observation notes, drawing a line down the middle of your paper and using these two categories keeps you mindful of when you are describing and when you are interpreting. The goal is to be aware always of the differences between the two.

On a new sheet of paper, draw a line down the middle and label the left "Descriptions" and the right side "Interpretations." Then use the chart to sort your observation notes from the activity above. Which ones have the details of what actually happened? Which ones have your interpretation of what might have been going on? Don't worry about keeping the sentences together—you may find that the first half of a sentence was an observation and the second half was a reflection. That's okay.

DESCRIPTIONS	INTERPRETATIONS
• A child (looks about two) is sitting on the floor holding his shirt up with his right hand exposing his bare belly.	
• He has a black marker clutched in his left hand and he is making black marks around his belly button.	• He is exploring how the marker feels and looks on his body.
• His head is tilted forward as he intently watches himself make the black marks on his body.	• He is making some kind of picture or purposeful marks just around his belly button.
• In the next photo the child is holding up his shirt and you can see marker streaks across his belly and on his chin. He is sucking his lower lip in.	• He looks like he might be worried that he has done something wrong.

Recognize the Components of Observation Skills

To discover the meaning of an observation, you need to have descriptive details to support your interpretations. Detailed information helps you discover possible interpretations and misinterpretations from your own filters and bias. The more details, information, and points of view that you uncover, the more options you can generate for responding to the children.

You can learn to observe for the detail. It requires you to notice when you are interpreting and to look closely for the smaller parts that make up the whole. When you find yourself interpreting, stop and ask, "What do I specifically see that leads me to this interpretation?" For example, while watching Coe use the markers in the photos above, our notes may say, "He is really interested in what he is doing." What do we specifically see that leads us to this interpretation of his interest? What in his actions, facial expressions, body language, or tone of voice are we interpreting as his interest?

Using these observation skills when we watch children reminds us to look conscientiously for the details of what we are seeing. Below is a list of these components, along with a definition of each, and, finally, an example of how to apply them in studying the photos of Coe.

Objectivity: Observing without judging. You put on hold your worry about mess and the possible reactions from Coe's mother.

> *Coe is holding up his shirt with his right hand, exposing his belly. In his left hand he is clutching a black marker, making black marks around his belly button.*

Specificity: Looking for specific details, such as the number of children and adults involved, the kinds and amounts of materials, and the time span of the activity.

> *Coe is alone on the floor right next to an easel that has a can of markers sitting in the trough. There are eight other children and two adults playing in the areas around him. He works for two to three minutes making marks around his belly button with a black marker.*

Directness: Recording direct quotes as much as possible. Still photos obviously don't offer sound, but observers can hear and record what children say.

> *After Coe put marks on his belly, he looked up and around, and quietly said, "No, no."*

Mood: Describing the social and emotional details of a situation. These include tones of voice, body language, facial expressions, hand gestures, and other non-verbal information. Mood clues can be difficult to decipher because we have an automatic, unconscious response to them. We have learned to "read" mood clues from infancy, and our memories of those early years don't have language associated with them. It takes considerable practice to learn to use mood cues for descriptive details rather than interpretations.

> *Coe works quietly with his head tilted forward as he intently watches himself make the black marks around his belly button.*

Completeness: Describing incidents as having a beginning, middle, and end. A complete recording describes the setting, who was involved, the action in the order it occurred, the responses, interactions, and the ending.

Coe, a two-year-old boy, sits alone on the floor of a toddler classroom while eight children and two adults work and play in various areas around him. He holds up his shirt with his right hand, exposing his bare belly. He has a black marker clutched in his left hand as he makes marks around his belly button. He finishes making the marks, then gets up, looks around, and says quietly, "No, no."

Saying, "Coe was really interested in exploring the markers," is not a story worth telling. In fact, if his mother is upset about the black marker all over his belly, then Coe deserves your advocacy on his behalf. If you told his mother the depth of this experience for Coe, with all of the details you noticed, you might be able to marvel together at this remarkable childhood moment. It might be easier for her to understand why you didn't stop him. Using observation skills to assemble the details of Coe's story reveals the richness of his activity. As more and more details come to light, you will notice that these seemingly ordinary and sometimes annoying childhood moments offer important opportunities for children to wonder and learn about themselves and the world they live in.

Practice Describing the Details

You can also practice noticing details in experiences unrelated to children. This activity can serve as a self-assessment of your skills in describing details. For this activity you will need another person and two identical sets of small building blocks or toys.

1. Sit back to back with a partner. Each person should have one of the sets of blocks or toys.
2. Build a structure or arrange a design with your blocks.
3. Describe to your partner the building or design you have made. Your partner must try to duplicate the building or design by listening to your directions without looking at what you have done. Neither of you should ask questions.
4. When you have finished, look together at the outcome. Discuss what worked and what didn't work about the direction giving.
5. Switch roles and have the other person take the lead. Follow the same procedures, but see if what you learned from the first round can help you in this round.
6. When you are finished, consider the differences between the two rounds of building.

Discuss the following questions.

– What happened? What did you discover?
– What success did you have? What did each of you do that helped you succeed?
– What hindered your ability to accomplish this task?
– What else would have helped?

Did you discover that this was a difficult or easy task for you? The task is meant to help you notice the importance of sharing similar understandings and agreed-upon meanings when communicating. Also, the more specific the descriptive details you used, the more likely you were to communicate the directions successfully. You probably found that your interpretations, especially without interaction and feedback, led to misunderstandings. When you collect observations and discuss the details together, rather than operating from individual opinions and interpretations, you have a better chance of understanding the complexity of what you're seeing, which makes you more effective.

Take Another Look

Once you become aware of the influences on what you see and how easy or hard it is for you to notice and describe details, you are on the road to improving your observation skills. The last activity of sitting back to back and trying to build what is being described also helps you assess your listening skills. Your ability to hear and see clearly will improve with each step you take to identify what shapes your perceptions. Notice how mood cues may impact your ability to be objective. Identify what you need to overcome as well as what you need to sharpen. Here are some further activities to move you along in this process.

More Exploration of Mental Filters and Their Influences on Perception

Go to an airport, park, or mall with a friend or colleague and sit on a bench together to people-watch. Talk together about what you see, challenging each other to give specific details rather than interpretations. Discuss the differences in what you notice as well as how and why you interpret what you see the same or differently. Write a reflection paper on what you discovered.

More Observation Practice—Putting It All Together

Try this activity either alone or with a partner or small group to get more practice collecting details, describing what you see, and interpreting your observations.

1. Gather more still photos. The black-and-white photography book, *The Family of Children,* is an excellent resource of photos of children with lots of action and emotions portrayed. Still photos are an easier starting place for practice than live-action videos.

2. To help you make the distinction between descriptions and interpretations, put a line down the center of some paper, labeling one side "descriptions" and the other "interpretations." You might also want to make a separate area for your "parking lot" to jot down your quick reactions and labels.

3. Write down what you see in the pictures and put your words and phrases under the category they belong to.

4. Review the Components of Observation Skills above to practice describing more details from your photos.

The more you practice these skills, the better you will get at observing. Once you have ample practice with the still photos, follow the same process with short video clips of children. Then practice with children in real life. Remember to take your time to really see children. Don't worry about a right answer or perfect writing skills.

More to Do

You've completed the first observation study session! You probably will agree that developing this approach and the required skills will take time and more practice. Some of your practice should focus on activities that will sharpen your ability to change perspectives, let go of your filters and "comfort zone," and feel more at ease with the disequilibrium that comes in letting go of your usual ways of looking at things. Included here are a few Art of Awareness activities to try as well as references for finding more. These suggestions are not directly related to observing children, but rather fun experiments that can help you develop flexible thinking—which, of course, has everything to do with your work with children.

Optical Illusions

Which of the horizontal lines in the image below are parallel? How do you know?

Source: *Great Book of Optical Illusions,* by Gyles Brandreth (New York: Sterling Publishing Company, Inc., 1985). Reproduced with permission. © Exploratorium® www.exploratorium.com

Do you see an old woman or a young one in this picture? Both images are present if you look closely. With effort you can switch back and forth from one image to another. Notice the disequilibrium that happens as you make the switch. Practice switching rapidly back and forth between each of the opposing images until you can do it comfortably.

Isometric Perspective Designs

Spend some time using colored pencils or markers to color in this design. Notice the changes in perspective you have to make as you work. Study your completed work to continue to practice shifting your perspective.

Source: *Isometric Perspective Designs and How to Create Them,* by John Locke (New York: Dover Publications, Inc., 1981). Used by permission.

Magic Eye 3-D Designs

Locate some Magic Eye postcards, calendar pictures, or books, such as *Magic Eye: A New Way of Looking at the World* (Kansas City, MO: N.E. Thing Enterprises, 1993). You can also check out a Magic Eye Web site at www.magiceye.com. Put the design right up to your nose and very, very slowly pull it away from your face. Look through the image without focusing on it. Try not to blink, and you will discover a hidden image that will magically appear. The key here is to let go of the expectation of seeing something. Only when you do this and really look into the design will an image appear. This is a tricky but useful activity to practice letting go of expectations to see what actually appears.

Spot the Difference/Find the Details

The ability to see details and distinctions does not come easily, nor without practice. A fun way to develop these skills is through the use of spot-the-difference children's books. You can do them alone or with a partner. There are many of these books available in libraries and bookstores. Here is a list of a few favorites:

- I SPY from Scholastic Books. There are several of these books available. They challenge you to find specific objects among a myriad of objects based on a theme or a riddle.
- *Look: The Ultimate Spot-the-Difference Book,* by A. J. Wood, illustrated by April Wilson (New York: Puffin Pied Piper, 1992). At first glance the lush pictures on facing pages seem identical; but take a closer look, and discover fascinating differences.
- *Metamorphosis: The Ultimate Spot-the-Difference Book,* by Mike Wilks (New York: Penguin, 1997). This is a much more complex spot-the-difference book. It has illustrations and text to compare on facing pages. Adding to its complexity, the underlying theme throughout the book is the cycle of life.

Reflect on Shifting Perspectives

After using any of the resources listed here, do some reflective writing about what you discovered. Here are some examples of teacher reflections.

At first try most of these activities make me feel dizzy and give me a headache. But once I work with them I can feel my brain getting settled, and I am able to have more control of the way I shift back and forth between images. It's so true that we don't like to have our views upset. I can see why we try so hard to stick to our own "truths" even in the face of contradictions.
—**Gail, preschool teacher**

These activities really made me look at what I take for granted as truth from my own stereotypes. I realize that looking for details is very important, and I should not just assume that I know what's going on at first glance.
—**Nicole, ECE student**

Recommended Resources

Carroll, Colleen. *How Artists See Animals.* New York: Abbeville Publishing Group, 1996. This is one in a series of books about how artists see in order to create their art. The author takes you through questions to guide your thinking as you look closely at various paintings, photographs, sculptures, and other art forms to see and interpret with the eye of an artist.

Wexler, Jerome. *Everyday Mysteries.* New York: Dutton Children's Books, 1995. This is a collection of photos of surfaces, silhouettes, cross sections, and edges. Viewed in different ways, everyday things become everyday mysteries. Here are photo puzzles vivid with color, pattern, shape, texture, and beauty. The object is to look closely to see if you can figure out what the objects are.

Wood, John Norris. Illustrated by Kevin Dean and John Norris Wood. *Nature Hide and Seek: Jungles* or *Nature Hide and Seek: Oceans.* New York: Alfred A. Knopf, 1987. Test your power of observation. See how many creatures you can find in the lush, detailed drawings of jungle or ocean flora and fauna.

3

STUDY SESSION

Observing for Children's Perspectives

If you have a child of two or three, let her give you beginning lessons in looking. Ask the child to come from the front of the house to the back and closely observe her small journey. It will be full of pauses, circling, touching, and picking up in order to smell, shake, taste, rub, and scrape. The child's eyes won't leave the ground and every piece of paper, every scrap, every object along the way will be a new discovery. It does not matter if this is familiar territory, the same house, the same rug or chair. To the child, the journey of this particular day, with its special light and sound has never been made before. So the child treats the situation with the open curiosity and attention that it deserves. The child is quite right.

Corita Kent

Learning Goals for This Study Session

In this study session you will

- Practice looking closely at the things around you
- Recall and reflect on a favorite childhood memory
- Study the components of childhood
- Practice seeing the children's perspectives and capabilities

Reflect on the Quote

Corita Kent reminds us that it is valuable for adults to remember the world from a child's point of view. Reread the quote above with these questions in mind:

- What is your reaction to this quote?
- Do you have any recent experiences that you can relate to it?
- What have you learned or been reminded of by a child that you wouldn't have noticed if that child hadn't shown or told you?

Read this teacher's reflection to spark your thinking and discussion about this quote.

> To me this quote means this: I go about my daily life rather quickly. A lot of times it involves going the same route, walking the same street, greeting the same people, and passing the same houses, trees, or flowers. As I keep my eyes straight ahead and my mind a million miles away I miss the small wonders of every day, the wonders that really make life precious. If I take off my blinders and my filters, the detail and the wonder will fill my senses and I will truly see! When I'm with children I will observe and take in the small wonders of what the children are doing and seeing, and I'll know I've seen something truly precious. —**Sherry, early childhood education (ECE) student**

Art of Awareness Activity

Looking Closely: Take a walk around outdoors. Approach this walk as if you are seeing things for the first time the way Corita Kent describes a child's journey in the quote above. Keep your attention on the ground. Pause, circle, touch, and pick things up to smell, taste, rub, scrape, or bend them. Notice shadows, light, and sounds. Choose something you are drawn to and spend a few extra minutes exploring it. Draw a sketch of it and write a description of all of the aspects of it and your reactions to it. Talk with a partner about what you discover.

Learn to See Childhood As a Significant Part of the Life Cycle

Children see so much that we miss. In fact, once we are adults, we miss out on most of who children are and the value of childhood. Even parents and teachers who spend each day with children often focus on who they will become, rather than who they are in the here and now. If we are to overcome this tunnel vision, we must start to notice and remember the remarkable point of view of a young child and the important work of childhood.

Given the short time they have been in the world, children are constantly demonstrating what they have learned and what they know how to do. Their expressions may seem naive or undeveloped, but in fact, they represent an incredible urge to make sense of the world. The more we learn about child development, and particularly the newest implications of brain research, the more it's confirmed that childhood is a profoundly significant time of life.

As we observe children pursuing an interest in their play and conversations, we have to recognize that these moments are the mortar and brick of a developing life. Being able to witness and participate in this process provides adults with a larger view of ourselves in the life cycle. Our lives are enriched and expanded when we pause to appreciate the experience of childhood.

When we take time to recall favorite childhood memories of our own, we value more fully what we see children doing. It is useful to think back to fond memories of your childhood regularly, for they provide continual insight into what children need from you. The next activity offers you this opportunity.

Practice with a Favorite Childhood Memory

You can do this activity on your own, with a partner, or with a small group. First, gather your thoughts and recall a favorite memory from your childhood. Use the following questions to help you explore the details:

- Where did this memory take place?
- What was in the environment?
- What were the sensory aspects of this place?
- What did it look like, smell like, sound like, feel like, taste like?
- Who was there?
- What feelings do you associate with this memory?
- What was your sense of time?
- What skills and competencies were a part of this experience that have influenced who you are today?

As you reflect on your memory, and perhaps hear those of others, consider the themes that are there. Most people share some of the following common elements from their childhood memories:

- Spending time outdoors with nature and or animals
- Being inventive, transforming found objects into props for play
- Taking risks, wanting power, adventures, and physical challenges
- Having lots of time to explore without adult interference
- Getting messy, dirty, and sometimes into mischief
- Working alone and with others, solving problems and resolving conflicts
- Being involved in meaningful work, often with adults
- Enjoying celebrations and family or community gatherings

It's not surprising that these themes come up among adults over and over again. These are some of the most significant experiences of childhood. They influence children's development and learning, so it is important for teachers to be able to recognize and value them. One of the easiest ways to recognize the value they have for children is to remember the value they had for us when we were children. As you become a keen observer of the children you work with, you will also see the value of these experiences for them.

Remembering our own childhood helps us keep it at the center of our thinking and planning. It helps us to uncover the child's point of view in the observations we make.

Observation Practice

Here are a couple of observation stories to help you practice uncovering the child's point of view.

Dancing with Shadows

Tiana, four months old, is propped on some pillows in a cozy corner of the infant room. Every day about this time the sun comes streaming in, creating a dance of shadows from the mobile hung in the window. Tiana seems content and relaxed, almost mesmerized as her eyes follow the shadow dance on the wall.

From time to time a larger shadow looms, covering the mobile shadow as a car or person passes by outside the window. Whenever this happens Tiana begins a dance. She waves her arms and legs rapidly as her dark eyes grow wide and her whole body leans forward with eager attention. "There it is again," she seems to be saying.

As you picture this moment with Tiana, reflect on these questions in writing or with a partner or small discussion group.

– How does Tiana show us her interest in the shadows?
– What clues does she give about the differences she notices with the shadows?

– What might she be understanding or trying to figure out with this shadow exploration?

Although babies don't use words, they have many ways of telling us what they are noticing and trying to understand. Tiana uses gestures as her language, showing us the attention to detail she has by making changes in her body. Grown-ups often overlook these seemingly small experiences for babies, when in fact, close observation shows us the complexity of what is going on.

From the time they are born and maybe before, babies are naturally equipped to use their ever-developing skills to learn about the world around them. They are also powerful communicators in calling our attention to their needs and interests.

Some adults have to discipline themselves to pay attention to these small moments. Others are easily drawn to these expressions of a baby's experience. Which is true for you? What might help you begin to notice more?

Making Things Right

Valerie, who is seven years old, goes through the same routines each day when she gets to her after-school program. First she goes around and greets everyone, addressing them with their first and last names with a monotone cadence: "Rhonda Black," "Pam Verner," "Tracy Custer." She then checks all the doors in the room, and if any of them are open, she closes them. On the days when the lights are off, she turns them on. Once she has completed these tasks she goes to the swings and stays there as long as the teachers will let her.

Though she doesn't have close friendships or get involved in activities with others, the children know that she is able to read and write and call her over to assist them. She responds to their requests to write or read to them, but that is the extent of her interactions and then she returns to her solitary activity. Typically this means connecting all the wooden train tracks together until every piece is used.

Look closely at the details of this story to see what you can learn about Valerie.

– What are some consistent patterns in her behavior?
– What is she good at?
– What does she seem to enjoy?
– What can you say about her relationships with others?

Do some reflective writing or discussing to explore Valerie's capabilities and perspectives.

Valerie has been diagnosed as an autistic child, but falling back on this diagnosis can lead to missing who she is and ignoring what she knows and can do. While it's true children like Valerie need some special consideration, the starting point for working with any child should be recognizing the way she sees the world and the strengths she brings to herself and others.

If your response to Valerie is one of irritation or a desire to control her, can you transform it to one of curiosity and eagerness to know more about how the world looks through her eyes? What questions might you ask yourself to help you focus on her capabilities?

My Life As a Dog

José spent almost the entire playtime (well over an hour) being a doggie. He crawled everywhere, across the room, into various nooks, exploring different areas of the room. Sometimes he pulled himself up briefly to a piece of furniture to see what others were doing, but he always hastily returned to his hands and knees to continue his doggie behavior.

Initially, a few other children were also on the floor meowing and crawling in catlike behavior. But this lasted no more than a few minutes, and they were on to something else. José stuck with it for the whole time, mostly on his own, but with very ingenious ways of interacting with others. Sometimes he snuggled the full length of his body up to someone's feet or legs. He used a variety of sounds to get attention, and in fact, hold brief conversations.

Many distinctive body motions and sounds were part of José's play. He whined, barked, growled, and showed his teeth. He shook his head and his behind back and forth. There were different actions for different people he came across, sometimes offered as a simple "Hi, what are you doing?" or a clear "Stay away from me." When he saw objects he liked or disliked, a doll, block, or puzzle piece, he did the same thing.

At one point he truly found a dog friend. His eyes met those of another child, and they seemed to immediately recognize that they were of the same species. They spent the next fifteen minutes moving back and forth across one area of the room with ever more complex sounds and motions bonding them as fast friends and playmates who knew how to teach each other things. They could invent ways of spending time together and enjoy each other's company.

Use the following questions to focus on José's experience in this observation:

– What is the essence of this experience from José's point of view?
– What does José know and know how to do?
– What is José exploring, experimenting with, or trying to figure out?
– What does José find frustrating?
– How does José feel about himself?

A first impression of José's doggie play may be that he is immature and unable to engage in any significant learning activity. But a closer look reveals how much he is communicating about what he knows and wants. José has found a way to explore the classroom and the range of materials, activities, and playmates it contains. Though he hasn't developed more formal skills in entering in this play, he has invented an engaging way to include himself. He demonstrates an understanding about how to communicate a range of feelings and interests.

At four years old José shows us he has closely observed dogs and knows the details of how they behave and express themselves. He knows other children are interested in this as well, and this is a way to connect with them. Indeed, he is quite successful in finding a playmate who can meet him at his level and take this play further.

When you look closely and examine the details of their actions from their point of view, you discover how ingenious and motivated children are to learn and connect with others.

Take Another Look

Each day in your teaching you have the opportunity to notice children's competence and creativity, even when they are engaging in annoying activities. If you approach your time with them as a researcher, filling your mind with questions rather than labels or judgments, you will discover a new way of seeing them. As you begin to cultivate this mindset, try the following activities to heighten your awareness.

Reflect on the Quote

On your own, with a partner, or with a small group reflect on the following quote: What's your view of children? Do you see them as the author does or in a different way?

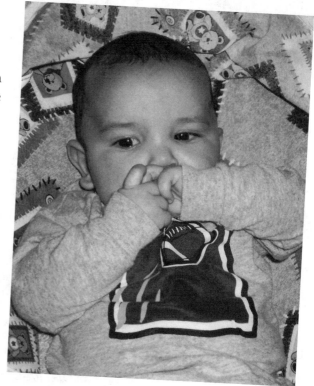

> *Children are capable, competent, curious, and creative. They are natural researchers as they question what they see, hypothesize solutions, predict outcomes, experiment, and reflect on their discoveries. Children are not passive, empty vessels waiting to be filled; rather, they are self-motivated learners actively seeking to understand the complex world in which they live. They are intrinsically motivated to learn and can be trusted as partners in curriculum development. Learning is therefore an ongoing, flexible, open-ended process wherein children construct their own understanding. Teaching is not telling; teaching is guiding discovery.* —**Lynn Staley**

Staley reminds us of our first task when trying to make meaning from our observations. We must ask ourselves, What are the children in any given observation showing us about their capabilities and curiosities? What are their hypotheses and predictions, their feelings and desires?

Practice Taking the Child's Perspective

Observe a child in your setting who is involved in ordinary self-directed play. Use the questions below to help you understand the child's perspective.

– What is the essence of this experience from the child's point of view?
– What does this child know and know how to do?
– What is this child exploring, experimenting with, or trying to figure out?
– What does this child find frustrating?
– How does this child feel about herself?

More Things to Do

It will take continual practice to cultivate these ways of seeing and being with children. Here are activities to contribute to your development.

Explore Your Current View of Children

Read the following statements and look at the accompanying photo, alone or with others, and explore how you typically see children. Consider which of these statements comes closest to representing your view. There is no right answer here and in many ways, each of them is true. Just reflect on which view most guides your behavior.

– Children are vulnerable and need protection.
– Children do fine on their own and adults should stay out of their way.
– Children need strong guidance and direction from adults in their lives.
– Children benefit from adults who both support and challenge them.

What are some of your specific behaviors that reflect your view of children? Are you comfortable with how you view children? Is it serving you well and keeping you interested and growing in your job?

Explore Images of Childhood in Children's Literature

From *Winnie-the-Pooh* to *Oliver Twist,* images of childhood engage our imaginations and emotions. They also can help us deepen our commitment to providing rich childhood experiences in our programs. Find a selection of children's literature to study. Compare three or four books, on your own or with others. As you reflect on each story, consider the following questions:

– What elements of childhood are portrayed in this story?

– How is this experience contributing to the children's sense of self and belonging?

– What elements from this story do you want to create for the children you work with?

Recommended Resources

Greenman, Jim. *Places for Childhood.* Redmond, Washington: Child Care Information Exchange, 1999. The essays in this book offer a lovely and practical picture of how programs can be places that value childhood.

Greenspan, Stanley I., and Nancy Thorndike Greenspan. *First Feelings. Milestones in the Emotional Development of Your Baby and Child.* New York: Viking, 1989. This book helps the reader recognize the central developmental stages of a child's emotional development and how to nurture it.

Stern, Daniel. *Diary of a Baby. What Your Child Sees, Feels, and Experiences.* New York: Basic Books, 1990. The author creates engaging stories of various experiences of a child from infancy through preschool years as the child might describe them in the child's own voice.

4

STUDY SESSION

Observing How Children Use Their Senses

Being with a child is largely a matter of becoming receptive to what lies all around you. It is learning again to use your eyes, ears, nostrils, and fingertips, opening up the disused channels of sensory impression. For most of us knowledge comes largely through sight, yet we look about with such unseeing eyes that we are partially blind. One way to open your eyes to unnoticed beauty is to ask yourself, "What if I had never seen this before? What if I knew I would never see it again?"

Rachel Carson

Learning Goals for This Study Session

In this study session you will

- Reawaken your ability to observe with all of your senses
- Examine closely with jeweler's loupes
- Practice seeing the details of children's sensory exploration
- Delight in and learn from children's use of their senses

Reflect on the Quote

Rachel Carson urges us to look at our ability to use our senses and see the world as a child does. Use the following questions to reflect on the quote:

– What do you think of this notion?
– What experiences do you have that relate to the ideas in the quote?
– How do you think it relates to your work with children?

Discuss your ideas with a partner or small group, or do some reflective writing. You might want to use this teacher's response to spark or extend your thinking.

As adults, most of us no longer think of the world as a mysterious place, and we look at the things around us with either a numb passiveness or critical judgment. Children view the world in such a different way. It is important for us to realize that children do not see things as we see them. And what a blessing it is for us to look at things in another way. It's sad that we have lost our sense of wonder, but it would be even sadder if we never noticed it was gone. We owe it to ourselves and the children we work with to close our "old" eyes and open new ones. —**Leslie, ECE student**

Art of Awareness Activity

Seeing Up Close: Here's an activity to practice looking at the world as if you've never seen it before. It can give you a sense of what it's like to see something unusual, and it can give you more practice in looking closely. This activity comes from *The Private Eye: Looking/Thinking by Analogy,* by Kerry Ruef. This K–12 curriculum is full of activities that use jeweler's loupes to observe the world in expanded ways. We suggest you get a jeweler's loupe either from the Private Eye folks (see Recommended Resources at the end of this chapter) or from your local eyeglass store. You could also use a high-powered magnifying glass, though it won't offer as focused a field of vision.

Follow these directions for seeing and exploring the world available to you with this simple tool.

1. Put the large end of the loupe or a magnifying glass up to your eye. Hold the object you want to examine, moving it closer and farther from your eye until it becomes focused. Forget the label or name of what you are looking at and see only the intricate details, colors, and textures.

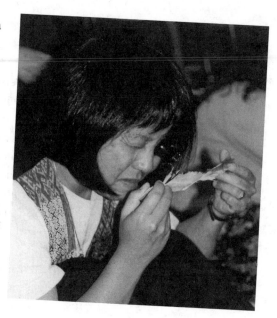

2. Write or describe the details of what you see.
3. Draw a sketch of what you are actually seeing. Don't try to make it look like something you know the name of.
4. Reflect on and talk or write about what it reminds you of.

Here is an example of a loupe drawing and description from a teacher in an observation class.

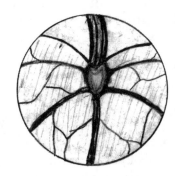

This is the part of a leaf where the stem meets the green leaf part. I could see all the veins very clearly. It kind of looked like a river system. The veins also looked like spiders' legs.

Learn to See Childhood As a World of Magic and Discovery

In the early childhood field we often talk about sensory exploration. Our classrooms have "sensory" tubs and tables, lots of recipes, curriculum guides, and resources for "sensory learning." Still, and understandably so, most often our adult response to children's sensory exploration is, "What a mess!" Left to their own devices, children will mix, spill, splash, bang, crash, take apart, and widely spread the stuff of the world. When we spend our days with groups of children, it seems easier to stop them in their tracks. After all, restraining this sensory exploration means less mess, less noise, fewer germs spreading, less work, and fewer parent complaints. But read what Helen Keller said about senses, and think again:

> *Smell is a potent wizard that transports us across thousands of miles and all the years we have lived. The odors of fruits waft me to my southern home, to my childhood frolics in the peach*

orchard. Other odors, instantaneous and fleeting, cause my heart to dilate joyously or contract with remembered grief. Even as I think of smells, my nose is full of scents that start awake sweet memories of summers gone and ripening fields far away.
—**Helen Keller**

The experiences children have in sensory exploration provide vital discoveries about themselves and the world they live in. These experiences are momentous for children because as they drink in the rich sensory information around them, their brain pathways are making the connections that will be the foundation for a lifetime of learning. As Helen Keller suggests, our senses are the way we come to know about the richness of life, in the past and present. The more of these experiences children have, the better.

Adults have busy lives filled with "To Do" lists, schedules, and deadlines. We rush around thinking we don't have time to "stop and smell the roses" or marvel at a sunset. We abandon our senses as we continually live in the past or the future, rather than in the present with our whole selves. If we are going to value these experiences and provide them for children, we have some work to do as grown-ups. We must reawaken our ability to use our senses to see the world. When we keep our own senses alert, we will more easily see and delight in a child's point of view. We will retain the best of our childlike qualities and stay fully alert in our adult bodies.

Practice Reawakening Your Senses

Use the following activity to open yourself up to your senses. You can do it alone, with a partner, or in a small group. Each person should look for four or five different, interesting objects that you have in your bags, pockets, or purses. Arrange the objects so you will be able to explore them easily. Try to let go of the name, identity, use, or description of the objects, and look at them as if you've never seen them before. Use the following guidelines to focus your exploration.

– Notice how many different sounds you can make with these objects. Keep track of how many you discover and list them.
– Explore all of the different ways these objects are affected by light. Look for sparkles, shiny surfaces, reflections, refraction, transparency, and translucency.
– Touch the objects and list as many words as you can to describe the textures and tactile feelings you notice. Use more than your hands for touching.
– Move the objects in as many ways as you can think of.
– Discover as many ways as you can to change, transform, or combine the objects (take things apart, stack, squish, pile, knock over, and so on).

Write a reflection of what you did to explore the objects and the new insights or discoveries you gained from this experience. As you read the following observation of children involved in sensory exploration, see if the above practice has enlivened your senses so that this observation takes on new meaning and appreciation.

Observation Practice

Here's a teacher's observation of sensory play in her room for you to practice on.

Bubble Symphony

As Shelby enters the room today she is immediately drawn to the sensory table, which is filled with warm, sudsy water, clear containers, funnels, and a variety of lengths and widths of clear, plastic tubing. She touches the water tentatively with her fingertips and coos, "Oooooh, warm," as she plunges both hands and arms up to her elbows. She gently swishes the water back and forth through the table, watching as the suds move on top of the small waves her motion creates. She places a funnel into the top of a tube, fills a cup, pours the foamy mixture in, and watches as the water flows out. "Look," she exclaims, pointing to the inside of the tube, "the bubbles are sticking."

Using her cup Shelby intentionally scoops the suds off the top of the water and tries to pour the mixture into the tube. Some of it sticks to the top of the tube, while the rest drips down the sides. Shelby puts her mouth to the tube and softly blows. The suds move toward the bottom and a newly formed bubble appears at the end. "Bubbles!" Shelby exclaims.

She sticks the end of the tube into the water and begins to blow gently, making a humming sound. She watches as the water jumps in response to her gentle breath, creating masses of cascading bubbles spilling over each other. Several children who have been working near her at the table follow her lead and begin to blow bubbles in the water and hum as they work. For several minutes they follow each other's lilting, "oooooohhhhhing" sounds and rhythms. As they work in unison, their music is soothing and calming, a magical Bubble Symphony!

Reflect on your own or talk with a partner or small group about your reactions to this story.

- What do you think the essence of the water and bubble experience was from these children's points of view?
- What can you tell about what they understand and know how to do?
- What do they seem to be exploring, experimenting with, or trying to figure out?
- Describe an example of when you have observed children involved in this kind of sensory experience.

What do you see when you watch children involved in scenes like these? Do you think about the spread of germs, the mess, or the noise? Do you take sensory play seriously? Do you see the learning that is taking place as the children work with math concepts, science and physics, small motor skills, social skills, and cooperation?

Of course, identifying the learning that occurs in sensory play is a useful consideration, but more important, do you see these joyful moments of childhood and value the delight, wonder, and magic they hold for children? Did you see the rich detail of the children's involvement with the water in the Bubble Symphony? In this small moment these children had the wonderful experience of sharing each other's way of being in the world. They were soothed and connected through their senses in the following ways:

- The sounds of humming together
- The smell of the clean, soapy water
- The feel of the warm, moving liquid on their hands and arms
- The sight of the waves rolling and sloshing, a smooth flat surface, then dripping and blowing and a lively, jumping design of drops and foam, water and bubbles

In the real world of early childhood programs children's sensory exploration can be exasperating and overwhelming to teachers. When a child dumps a container of water on the floor to watch the puddles form, and another paints all over himself because it feels good, and it's the third time today you've had to help a child change into dry clothes, you may not be able to appreciate the magic and wonder of such moments. If you adopt the general practice of observing closely with awareness, however, you will generally feel calmer and more nurtured as a teacher. This careful attention helps you mediate your own frustration and thus choose a response that will support the children's self-esteem and natural curiosity. Read the next observation with these ideas in mind.

A Glitter Path

Kohl (four years old) has spent the last few days in the block area carefully arranging the blocks in a long, curvy pathway. He is at it again today. The block path has S-shaped formations and covers the entire carpet of the block area. Kohl stops for a moment to look at the path. Then he goes to the art area and gets a large container of red glitter off the shelf. He kneels over the block path and takes pinches of glitter out of the container. With great concentration he slowly opens his fingers and lets go of the glitter. He intently watches the glitter flakes drift down to the blocks, his mouth starting to form the smallest of smiles. Kohl works diligently, forming a line of glitter along the entire length of the block path.

Reflect on your own or work with a partner or in a small group to discuss your reactions to this story.

– What is the essence of this experience for Kohl?
– What do you think he is trying to figure out as he uses the blocks and glitter in this way?
– How would you respond? Why?

Can you see Kohl's point of view in this story? Do you see this as a moment of magic as he watches the sparkly glitter float down to the blocks? Does his quest to cover the path of blocks with a path of glitter give you some insights into what understandings about the world he is pursuing? Is he working on some aspect of spatial relationships by revisiting his line-making in this way?

When we watch his strategies closely we see that they are practical as well as magical. In most settings it would not be workable for the teacher to let Kohl continue to pour the glitter all over the block area. Stopping him is a reasonable thing to do. In this case, the mess and cost of glitter will probably have to override his pursuit. But if you have observed attentively, you will have more appreciation of the moment, rather than just trying to stop it. You will have learned more about Kohl, his questions, and his curiosity. How might you intervene in a gentle, respectful way, sharing your admiration for his ideas and strategies, even as you explain that he cannot continue spreading the glitter?

Take Another Look

Children immerse themselves in sensory experiences because these activities encompass action and interaction. They are soothing, freeing, and full of possibility. Sensory materials feel magical to children as they manipulate and transform them. Children marvel at the things adults find ordinary, messy, or even boring. From their point of view, there are so many new things to look at, to hold in their hands, to rub, to taste, and to smell. These are the details we need to record and embrace so we can remind ourselves and others of some of the most meaningful and vital experiences in the lives of young children. Here are more activities to enhance your ability to see and delight in these sensory endeavors.

Reflect on the Quote

If you want to do something good for a child, give her an environment where she can touch things as much as she wants.
—**Buckminster Fuller**

Now that you've had the opportunity to awaken your own senses and to observe children's sensory play with a new awareness, consider the words of Buckminster Fuller. You can do reflective writing or discuss the quote with a partner or small group.

Observe Sensory Exploration

If you approach observing with heightened awareness, you learn to see the smallest details of children's sensory explorations. Challenge yourself to notice children using their senses in the block area, in the drama area, at the painting easel, on a field trip, during circle time. Observe in a real setting with children or view a short video clip. As you observe, practice noticing the details of their involvement and then find the meaning by looking for the children's point of view. What seems to be the essence of their experience? What do they seem to be exploring, investigating, or trying to figure out? What do they find pleasurable, comforting, or intriguing? Start with these photos:

Collect Descriptive Sensory Words

Because we are not accustomed to noticing details, our vocabulary to describe them is often limited. Here's an initial list of descriptive sensory words. Work alone or with others to brainstorm additional words to add to it. Keep this list handy and see if it helps you record the details and mood clues in your observations of children's sensory experiences.

Sight—shiny, glistening, shimmering, sparkly, gleaming, glowing, brilliant, dim, hazy, foggy, transparent, glowing, silvery, flashes, colorful, vibrant, faded, vivid, pale

Sound—crunch, crackle, sizzling, whirring, crash, thump, tinkle, whisper

Taste—salty, sweet, sour, spicy, oily, tart, bitter, savory

Smell—pungent, sweet, strong, musty, fresh, earthy

Touch—slimy, cold, icy, warm, cool, hot, prickly, soft, smooth, tingling, squishy, bumpy, gentle, rough, hard

Movement—glide, swoop, flutter, race, bubble, erupt, dodge, crash, bounce, speedy, graceful

More Things to Do

Here are more activities you can do on your own or with a partner to keep your senses alert and your awareness growing.

Play with Bubbles

Gather a variety of bubble-making objects such as pipes, wands, strawberry baskets, and coat hangers bent into different shapes. Make yourself a batch of bubble solution and spend at least thirty minutes blowing bubbles. Notice the shapes, sizes, colors, and rainbow reflections that your bubbles make. Try to make both really big bubbles and lots of very small bubbles. Chase and pop the bubbles you make.

BUBBLE SOLUTION RECIPE

- 1 part dishwashing liquid (Joy or Dawn works best)
- 1 part corn syrup or glycerin
- 3 parts water

Add the dishwashing liquid and the corn syrup or glycerin to the water and mix gently until thoroughly combined.

Use Your Nose

For an entire day be aware of all the odors and scents around you. Go out of your way to smell flowers and take deep breaths of the air. Pay attention to the odors both indoors and outdoors: natural smells, human-made smells, pleasant and unpleasant odors. As you come across different odors, pay attention to how they make you feel and react. Write or talk to a partner about your experiences.

Jeweler's Loupes

Explore at least ten more objects with the jeweler's loupe, writing a description of the details then drawing a sketch of it.

Recommended Resources

Ackerman, Diane. *A Natural History of the Senses.* New York: Vintage Books, 1990. This is an intriguing, knowledgeable, and compelling book on the science, mood, character, and geography of the human senses.

Carson, Rachel. *The Sense of Wonder.* New York: Harper and Row Publishers Inc., 1984 and 1990. This gorgeous book of photographs accompanies the wise observations and writings of the time Carson spent with her nephew Roger.

Ruef, Kerry. *The Private Eye: Looking/Thinking by Analogy.* Seattle, Washington: Private Eye, 1992. This is a terrific K–12 curriculum using observation with jeweler's loupes to generate language, scientific inquiry, and drawing to see. It's also a good source for low-cost jeweler's loupes. Contact them at: Private Eye, PO Box 646, Lyle, WA 98635; ph. 509-365-3007; fax 509-365-3777.

Self, Dana. *Intimate Landscapes: The Canyon Suite of Georgia O'Keeffe.* New York: Universe Publishing, 1997. A special compilation of the abstract watercolor paintings of Georgia O'Keeffe, accompanied by short excerpts from writers who capture similar sensory details in their descriptions.

5

Observing How Children Explore, Invent, and Construct

It is not necessary for the child to awaken to the sense of the strange and humorous by giving a man a luminous nose. To the child it is sufficiently strange and humorous to have a nose at all.

G. K. Chesterton

Learning Goals for This Study Session

In this study session you will

- Practice looking closely by doing "finder" drawings.
- Examine the importance of children learning to invent with open-ended materials.
- Explore and invent with open-ended materials or loose parts.
- Practice seeing the details of how children use open-ended materials.

Reflect on the Quote

Reflect upon the quote that opens this chapter. Do some reflective writing or discuss this with others, using the following questions as a guide:

– What do Chesterton's words mean to you?
– How do they relate to your work with children?

Consider what this teacher wrote:

Children look at everything in an exciting new way. Think of how exciting our lives would be if we looked at life with this different perspective. My daughter (age five) and I were on the way to my class last week and she was noticing the clouds as we drove. She noticed each one and how different they were from each other. We talked for 20 minutes about the clouds. Then she said, "When we meet Daddy I can tell him how exciting the clouds are." I was into my busy day, rushing to make it to class, and she made me see the beauty I was missing. This quote, and especially my daughter, are great reminders of how nice it is to think like a child. **—Kari, ECE student**

Art of Awareness Activity

Drawing with a Finder: In *Learning by Heart,* Corita Kent offers us another tool for looking closely. From scrap material she created a "finder" tool, which serves the same purpose as a camera lens or viewfinder. A finder helps take things out of context and allows you to practice seeing details without labels and judgments.

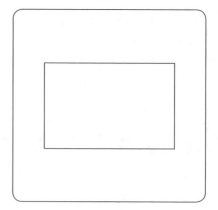

1. Create a finder for yourself. A quick way to do this is to use an empty 35-millimeter slide holder. You can also make your own finder by cutting a small rectangular hole (about the size of a 35-millimeter slide) out of a heavy piece of paper or cardboard.

2. Take your finder with you on a walk around the building or outside, anyplace where there is a lot to see. Look at the world through the finder for at least ten minutes. You can do this alone, or better yet, do it with a partner and discuss what you are noticing. Remember, the goal is to practice seeing details out of the context of their name or purpose.

3. Next, use your finder to frame a small section of a magazine or calendar picture. Observe carefully what is inside the small rectangle.

4. Using colored pencils or thin markers, draw what you see inside the triangle in an enlarged scale on an 8.5-by-11-inch piece of paper. By changing the scale you will notice the details in a new way. Your drawing will be a larger version of what is inside the rectangle. Metaphorically, this is exactly what we are trying to do in highlighting our observations of childhood's ordinary moments, enabling those moments to become more visible to us and to the larger society.

Learn to See Childhood As a World of Possibilities

Children have few preconceived notions about what the world ought to be like, about how they should feel, or what they must do according to prescribed formulas. They view the world as abundant with possibilities. Each day is filled with the excitement of new discoveries, rather than the pressing weight of obligations. Each minute and each activity is experienced as "now" rather than as a worried look into the future.

Unlike adults, young children have yet to develop permanent labels, automatic responses, or typical uses for most of the stuff they see all around them. They haven't learned the "right" answers or the "right" way to use things. This lack of experience and information can get them in trouble and put them in danger. Because of this, most adults see our role as protecting children from themselves. On the other hand, adults alternatively often see this innocence and ignorance as endearing and humorous. Children are viewed as "cute," and we chuckle when "kids say the darndest things."

But when we watch them with openness and respect, we cannot trivialize children in these ways. Close observation helps us see that childhood is filled with curiosity, creativity, and unlimited possibility. Children are born to dive in, take apart, rearrange, and invent, using whatever captures their imagination and curiosity for a whim or an intense purpose. As grown-ups we have a balancing act to do. We must offer the words and tools children need to make it safely in the world and provide multiple opportunities and materials to expand their curiosity and inventiveness. We must focus on their curiosity and investigation as much as we emphasize their safety and security so as not to squelch children's natural curiosity and their right to learn in their own effective ways.

The world of formal schooling and consumerism conspires against us in this work. The bulk of activities and materials made for and marketed to children are invented by someone else. Parents and teachers think they are helping children by buying them the latest fancy toy or curriculum package, only to watch children become quickly bored, looking for the next new toy or activity. All of us know the story of the child who plays longer with the gift box than with the toy inside. What children really need is an environment stocked with open-ended materials and loose parts, things from nature as well as the recycle bin. When we offer children these kinds of experiences, they become creators rather than consumers of their experiences.

We adults are also caught up in this consumer world. We no longer see ourselves as creators. Early childhood catalogues offer us prepackaged, prepared materials, things we previously invented for ourselves. The following activity can help you remember the difference. It may be difficult and uncomfortable at first, because we are so used to looking outside ourselves for answers. Stick with it to reclaim your own creativity and inventiveness.

Practice Exploring and Inventing with Loose Parts

Gather a collection of open-ended materials both from the recycle bin and from nature. Some suggested items to have in your collection include the following:

- Stones, shells, leaves, twigs, beach glass
- Cardboard tubes and small boxes
- Tiles, paint, and Formica samples
- Yarn, wool, twist ties
- Film canisters, plastic containers and lids, door hinges

Make sure you have many of each kind of item so there will be enough to explore and invent with. Work with a partner or small group so you can exchange ideas and reflections. Use the following guidelines to focus your attention and activity with the materials:

1. Explore the materials to discover how many ways you can sort and classify them, within the like groups as well as across the different groups.
2. Talk together and brainstorm at least one hundred ways you could use these materials, alone and in combination with each other. Try to break away from the typical uses for them and think about what else they might become.
3. Next use the materials to invent and construct something. You can do this alone or with others in your group. Draw on your explorations and discussions to inspire your invention.

When you have completed your inventions, use the following questions to reflect on your process.

- Think back to when you first began to sort and classify the materials. What were your thoughts as you first started working with the materials? What strategies did you use to decide on the categories? What did you discover about this process?

- Reflect on the brainstorming part of the activity. How did you generate ideas? What made it easy? What made it difficult?
- Discuss the invention process. How did you come up with your ideas? What was your group process? What helped the group work together? What hindered the group process? If you chose to work alone, discuss why you made that choice and how it was different from the group work.
- Think about the entire experience and how it relates to children's use of materials. What is the value of these kinds of materials? What do children gain when they are able to play in this way?

Try this activity more than once. Keep a collection of loose parts for yourself so you can turn to them often for sustaining your own creativity. Even further, watch children and get ideas from them about possibilities you never considered.

Observation Practice

Following the children's lead can teach you a lot about flexible, inventive thinking. Here are some sample observations that bear out this point.

Under the Cedar Tree

For the past month during outdoor time Sam, Lauren, and Eric have been playing together under the giant cedar tree. They sit together in a patch of dirt where a large root from the tree is poking out of the ground. Their ongoing visits to this spot are evident by the 3-foot-diameter hole that has been slowly getting bigger. Their daily routine is to find small twigs that become their digging tools. Then they sit around the hole together, poking and scraping, earnestly wearing away the compacted, rock-hard ground.

Many expeditions and adventures have unfolded as they dig. Today one of them has filled part of the hole with cedar branches that are still covered with needles.

Lauren: "This is our hideout. If we wait under here, the bad guys can't get us."

Sam: "Yeah, they can't get through the spikes. These spikes will keep them out. They'll be dead if they go through the spikes."

Eric: "We need more! Come on, get some more."

He quickly scans the area for more small branches. The others follow. They add more branches until the hole is totally covered.

Lauren: "We need some animals for in here. This can be their food too."

She has rediscovered the small pinecones that have fallen from the cedar tree. She gathers some and puts them in the hole under the branches.

Eric: "The animals can't get out. Quick, a volcano. It's exploding. The animals are flying out."

The others join in the excitement. Branches and pinecones fly all around the hole. Their eyes sparkle, and they laugh together as they throw the items into the air, letting them fall on their heads.

Lauren: "It's raining, it's raining."

They throw the materials up over and over again, running around in small circles, ducking and shaking things off as they fall.

Sam: "Let's dig some more. Let's make a bigger and bigger hole all the way to the sky."

They gather up more branches, break off some twigs, tear off the needles, and with these new tools go back to their digging.

Sample Observation: Rocket Blasters

The boys invented ways to attach the cardboard tubes to their bodies and called them "rocket blasters." They used elastic bands to tie them around their arms, legs, and backs. They used these props to enhance a space drama they were playing in the block area.

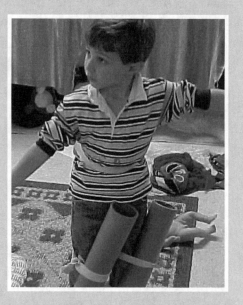

Toddlers and Tubes

Teacher Jamie decides to offer some new materials to her young toddlers today. She gathers together different lengths and varieties of tubes and PVC pipes, both cardboard and clear plastic. She also includes baskets, buckets, and a collection of balls. When the children notice the new materials they approach curiously but with caution. The exploration begins slowly. Jessica puts one ball into a clear plastic tube and looks up smiling. She stacks more balls on top until the tube is overflowing. Next she takes one of the buckets and fills it until it overflows with the plastic tubes.

Bryson begins to put the tubes inside each other. He discovers that only certain tubes will fit inside other tubes. Bryson picks up one of the long tubes and uses it first as a golf club to hit one of the balls and then swings it like a baseball bat, pretending to hit a ball.

The exploration and invention continues to unfold. Next, a group of the boys work together to line up the tubes from tallest to the smallest and begin to drop balls in each of them one by one. Laughing excitedly they knock the tubes over and the balls spill all over the rug. They exuberantly run to gather up the balls and begin filling the tubes again.

Other children use the tubes as viewfinders, looking through them at the room or at objects such as their hands. At one point Andrew puts his tube flat on the ground and lies down to look through the tube while he pushes a car through it. Charlie laughs hysterically as he looks through a giant PVC pipe. It frames his entire face!

Reflect on your own or work with a partner or small group to discuss the meaning of these observations. Use the following questions to guide your thinking:

– How did the children use the materials in their constructions and drama?
– What construction and building details did you notice?
– What inventions did they make?
– How did they use the materials to represent their ideas?
– What role did the materials play in their drama?
– What seemed to be the underlying themes of their drama?

When we look closely at these observation stories we can begin to answer these important questions. What role do the environment and materials play in the children's play and learning? What happens when children are able to enter into play from their own interests and developmental levels? What is the value of children playing with the same materials over time? How does the children's play help them acquire social skills and develop relationships?

Beyond their learning value, open-ended materials offer children experiences with what is possible, rather than what is "right." When you watch, listen, and support children's inventions with open materials, you see their total focus and intense drive to make their ideas and theories visible. You can watch the flexibility of their thinking as they figure out new ways to solve problems and accomplish their goals. You will see their delight in sharing and building on an idea with others. Watching children at work with open materials, you can understand how human beings with time, opportunity, purpose, and passion came to invent the wheel, build a community, compose a symphony, and fly to the moon.

Take Another Look

If you are working in a setting that hasn't previously made loose parts available to children, you will need to introduce them in a gradual way. Things like boxes from food packaging, paper towel and toilet paper tubes, and several rolls of masking tape make a good starting point. These are open-ended enough that children won't assume that you have something specific in mind to do with them. You can try modeling by using self-talk while picking up different pieces, saying things like, "This reminds me of…" Or, "If I wanted to make something that needed a long tube, I could use this." Once children begin to see that their ideas can be represented with the materials, they will begin to use them more freely.

Designate a specific area of the room for your recyclable "loose parts." Some teachers refer to this shelf or storage bin as "the inventor's box" or "the creation station." In their book, *Beautiful Stuff: Learning with Found Objects* (see Recommended Resources), Cathy Topal and Lella Gandini demonstrate how a studio space in a program was set up as part of a long-term project that involved families in gathering materials and children in sorting, organizing, and arranging them in an inviting way.

Offer Open-Ended Materials

Provide ample open-ended materials both from nature and the recycle bin for a group of children and watch how they use them. For preschool-age children and older, make sure you have enough items and materials they can use to attach things together, such as tape, twist ties, staplers, stickers, string, wire, and so on. With infants and toddlers, make sure the items have no small parts or pieces that may be dangerous to this age group.

Offer a selection of these materials every day for a week so you can see what happens over time. Observe attentively how the children use the materials and reflect on the following questions either alone or with a partner:

– What do the children do with the objects and materials?
– What seems to capture their interest?
– What seems to be fun and pleasurable?
– What experiences, people, and other materials do they seem to connect with these materials?
– How do they talk about the materials?

– How do they use the materials to represent their ideas, as both symbols and props and actual inventions and constructions of their ideas and play?
– How does their use of the materials change over time?

Observe the Use of Found Materials

Make note of how children use open-ended materials they may find on their own either in the classroom or outside. Reflect on what you see using the following questions:

– What open-ended materials or items did they find?
– How and where did they use the materials: for sensory exploration, for construction, for drama?
– What do the items have in common?
– How did the children use the materials to represent their ideas and understandings?

Sample Observation: Experimenting with the Ramp

Chloe and Lauren tried many strategies to position the ramp for an incline to roll the balls down. After securing it to the block shelf, the wall, and the cupboard, they realized the balls zoomed the fastest when they took turns holding the ramp at just the right angle.

More Things to Do

The idea of creating things from found materials isn't limited to young children. In fact, as you read about how artists, architects, and inventors develop, they often make use of some of these ideas and materials.

Try More Finder Drawings

Find more images to look through with your finder. Complete at least ten more finder drawings.

Observe Artists' Work

Here is an engaging activity that will help you see more details and look with the critical eye of an artist.

Visit an art gallery or collect photos or greeting cards that have paintings, drawings, sculptures, or other art forms on them.

Work on your own or with a partner or small group using the following questions to analyze the art together.

– What do you think the artist wanted you to notice about this artwork? Why?
– What part of the artwork most interests you? Why?
– Examine the different ways the artist used line and shape. Use your finger to trace them. As you do this, notice how they change and where they lead to and from.
– Describe the patterns, colors, textures, and objects in the artwork.
– How would you describe the mood of the artwork?

Recommended Resources

Brosterman, Norman. *Inventing Kindergarten.* New York: Harry N. Abrams, Inc., 1997. This is a comprehensive book about the origin of kindergarten and its founder, Friedrich Froebel. This beautifully illustrated book describes the successful system Froebel devised for teaching young children art, design, mathematics, and natural history with materials and methods that will be readily recognizable to early childhood teachers today.

Chaffee, John, Ph.D. *The Thinker's Way.* Boston, New York, Toronto, London: Little, Brown and Company, 1998. Chaffee offers steps to live mindfully in order to think and communicate more effectively.

Gelb, Michael J. *How to Think Like Leonardo DaVinci.* New York: Delacorte Press, 1998. This book describes DaVinci's practical approach to creative thinking and self-expression. It thoroughly explores seven principles that the author has drawn from extensive study of DaVinci and his work. Each principle is followed by suggested strategies for developing these principles in yourself.

Hirsch, E. S., ed. *The Block Book.* Washington, D.C.: NAEYC, 3rd edition, 1996. This is a classic book offering wonderful details about the learning that can occur with block building and how to provide for it.

Topal, Cathy Weisman, and Lella Gandini. *Beautiful Stuff. Learning with Found Materials.* Worcester, Massachusetts: Davis Publications, Inc., 1999. This is a visually captivating story of how one preschool program involved families in collecting loose parts and then turned them into a long-term organizing, exploring, and creative-constructions project. The photos alone support the value of using open-ended materials.

6

Observing How Children Connect with the Natural World

We don't understand the fullness of everything, of anything. Things constantly change and we may have seen an object only five minutes ago and thought we knew it, but now it is very different. To be able to adjust to these subtle differences means looking anew with what new materials we have gathered up inside ourselves, as well as noting what changes have taken place within the object. We need to be aware of what we don't know yet.

Corita Kent

Learning Goals for This Study Session

In this study session you will

• Reconnect with the wonders of the natural world.
• Learn from children's deep fascination and connection with nature and living things.
• Practice seeing the details of children's connections with the natural world.

Reflect on the Quote

Think over Corita Kent's words, using the following questions as a guide:

– Are there ways in which you are not the same person you were yesterday?
– Is there anything you look at today differently than how you saw it yesterday?
– What do you not yet know about the children you work with?

This requires some consideration of the details of what you were thinking, believing, knowing, and seeing yesterday as compared with today. Do some reflective writing and talk with another person or a group about your thinking. You might want to use these teacher responses to spark or extend your thinking.

This quote says in such a concrete way what I have been learning as I go through these study sessions. Living is an unfolding process. Nothing is ever set, done, or a final product. This is especially true for me as I spend my days with children. We are constantly changing. Although many of the feelings, issues, and situations we work through are similar each day, we always have new views and abilities to work with. It seems that each day grows from the day before to the next day, so it has some of what was but now is totally new. This is hard to explain. Corita Kent did it much more simply than I have, but I think I understand it more deeply than I can express it.
—**Jan, preschool teacher**

What this quote is saying to me is that we cannot just observe something for a short period of time. We need to study things for a longer period of time. The quote is about taking more time to sit down and enjoy the company of the children and look at the way the world looks to them. Their world is continually changing. They are changing so dramatically as they grow and develop. Something you saw five minutes ago could be changing right before your eyes. New understandings, new ideas, new inventions.
—**Travis, student teacher**

Art of Awareness Activity

Observing Nature: Try this activity adapted from Corita Kent's book *Learning by Heart.*

1. Choose something from nature to observe: a tree, a flower, the moon, a shadow, or a living creature, such as an insect or bird, your dog or your cat. Make sure you choose something that you can observe more than once.
2. Use the following guidelines to focus your observation:
   • Look at the shape and the parts that make up the whole of your subject.
   • Look for patterns and textures in the subject.
   • Look for dark and light shades.
   • Look for colors in the subject, subtle as well as vivid.
   • Look for the different ways the subject moves.
3. Observe your subject for at least fifteen minutes a day for a week. Write a list of the specific details you notice each day. If you like, you can make sketches to go with your notes.
4. Keep an ongoing collection of the details of your observations. Notice the differences in your observations and in yourself each time you observe.
5. At the end of the week get together with a partner or small group. Discuss the process you went through to study your subject. Share your discoveries about your subject and yourself.

Learn to See Childhood As a World of Natural Wonders

… [T]hat was the main thing about kids then: we spent an awful lot of time doing nothing.… All of us, for a long time, spent a long time picking wild flowers. Catching tadpoles. Looking for arrowheads. Getting our feet wet. Playing with mud. And sand. And water. You understand, not doing anything. What there was to do with sand was let it run through your fingers. What there was to do with mud was pat it, and thrust it, lift it, and throw it down.… My world, as a kid, was full of things that grownups didn't care about.
—**Robert Paul Smith**

This quote from Robert Paul Smith illuminates the way that as human beings we have an ardent desire for a place that helps us feel connected to the earth and the sky and other living creatures. For it is in these places that we feel a part of something bigger than ourselves.

Being outdoors is among the deepest, most passionate joys of childhood. There is the vastness of the sky and the intricacies of a leaf. In cities, the light bounces off buildings and creates shadows and reflections that are interesting to follow.

The outdoors has blustery windy days that stir our bodies and our imagination. It has gentle rain that glistens and makes puddles perfect for jumping and splashing. It has the sun, which warms our bodies and our spirits. It is full of creatures that scamper, fly, and slither. The outdoors is always changing and renewing itself. It is ripe for investigating and transforming and creating miniature worlds and dramas.

Outdoors children can be loud and boisterous, or quiet and contemplative. They can experience the life cycle, anticipate the changes in the seasons, and observe and care for living things. They can discover the different ways people live and work and play. Outdoors children can invent games, learn how to take care of themselves, and watch out for others. It is a place for spiritual connections and emotional and physical release.

Sadly, the majority of children growing up in early childhood programs have outdoor time limited by a daily schedule and the restrictions of a concrete playground with anchored, commercial toys that don't bend in the wind or change with the seasons. As the modern world gets bigger and fears about safety and liability grow, children have less and less opportunity to meet their critical human needs for connection with nature.

It is vital for adults who work in early childhood programs to recognize the profound importance of children making connections with the natural world. Observing children involved in these experiences is a way to inform and enlighten yourself. Remembering your own childhood experiences outdoors is another powerful tool for recognizing the significance of this with children.

Practice Remembering the Wonders of Nature

This activity will help you to continue to reconnect with the wonders of the natural world. Think about a place outdoors from your childhood where you loved spending time. Draw a simple map of this place, noting these features on the map:

- Things that were growing: trees, plants, grass, or gardens
- Living creatures you found there: animals, insects, reptiles, or birds
- Forms and structures both natural and human-made: water, rocks, stumps, hills, sheds, barns, porches, hideouts, water towers, or bridges
- Places where you played, what you played, and the materials you played with

When you have completed your map, share it and the stories it evokes with a partner or a small group. Compare the similarities and differences of one another's experiences. Discuss the value and importance these experiences have played in your life. Compare your experiences to those of the children you work with.

Observation Practice

Remembering your own experience and those you heard about in the discussion, consider these two observations of how children connect with the natural world. After each is a set of questions to reflect on.

First Frost

It was a brisk, icy morning when the children burst onto the play yard bundled in coats, hats, and mittens. As they headed through the gate, they suddenly stopped, noticing the sparkly frost glazing every surface of the yard: the grass, tire climber, sandbox, and swings. Everything was coated with a thin layer of twinkling white ice. Children started running to all parts of the yard testing the surfaces, shouting out to each other excitedly as they explored the enchanting landscape.

"Whoaa ... Look!" Rebecca sang out as she approached the tire climber. She gingerly touched the surface with her mittened finger. When she lifted it and looked, again she said, "Whoaa...!" marveling at the impression her finger left in the frost.

She picked one of the last fall leaves, carefully investigating the tiny crystals on the surface. Then she gathered up a collection of the leaves, examining each one and lining them up along the edge of the sandbox. Next she began rubbing and scraping the frosty layer off the wooden edge. At one point Rebecca slowly lowered her head to the edge, stuck out her tongue, and licked the frost. She looked up with a beaming smile and exclaimed, "It's cold!"

Rebecca jumped up and ran to join the other children who were stomping exuberantly through the grass, stopping and noticing each footprint they made with their movements. They followed each other's footprint trails, turning their wintry dance into a game of chase as the magical blanket melted under them.

Reflect on your own or with a partner or small group to find the meaning in this story. Use the following questions to guide your thinking and discussions:

– What do the children seem most interested in as they explore the frost?
– What strategies do they use to explore?
– What questions or theories can you see them pursuing in the details of their actions?

Watching children closely you will see their quest to connect to nature in any small way they can. It's heartening to discover that when given the least bit of opportunity, children find the natural world in their environment. They discover the crack in a sidewalk and chip away to uncover the pliable dirt. They are drawn to every puddle in the asphalt streets of urban environments. Or, as in the First Frost story above, they see magic and opportunity for discovery in the change of nature they experience around them. We must seize the opportunity to strengthen children's natural inclination to wonder and delight in the natural world.

In her book *The Sense of Wonder*, Rachel Carson offers us a powerful vision for children and for ourselves:

> *A child's world is fresh and new and beautiful. It is our misfortune that for most of us that clear-eyed vision, that true instinct for what is beautiful and awe inspiring, is dimmed and even lost before we reach adulthood. If I had influence with the good fairy who is supposed to preside over the christening of all children, I should ask that her gift to each child in the world would be a sense of wonder so indestructible that it would last throughout life, as an unfailing antidote against the boredom and disenchantment of later years, the sterile preoccupation with things that are artificial, the alienation from the sources of our strength.* —**Rachel Carson**

A Furry Friend

Three-year-old Matthew came into the room unable to figure out how to settle into playtime. His foray into the block area ended with two of the older boys yelling at him for knocking their building over. His response to this incident was to dump two baskets of small building toys all over the floor. The children protested in unison, "Matthew...!" The teacher asked him to come help her put the pieces away. When he refused, she held him on her lap while she put the pieces in the baskets.

Next Matthew went to the water table. He began splashing wildly, getting water all over three other children as they complained loudly, "Matthew...!" Matthew's clothes were soaking wet. When the teacher suggested that he needed dry clothes, he ran and hid under one of the tables. She coaxed him out and helped change his clothes.

Matthew found a place to sit at the playdough table where he immediately grabbed a rolling pin that another child was using. The child screamed at him and wrenched the rolling pin out of his hands. Matthew roared loudly in her face. He sat for a while poking at the playdough and then got up and quietly found his way to the empty classroom next door.

There, Matthew went straight to the large bunny cage sitting in the corner of the room. He bent over, opened the cage, and peeked inside. "Hi bunny," he whispered. The bunny hopped toward him, and he lifted it carefully out of the cage. Matthew huddled close to the bunny, cooing softly as he stroked its furry body and soft ears. He followed the bunny to the corner of the room and curled up with the bunny nestled against his body. He stayed for a long while lovingly watching, petting, and talking to his furry friend.

Keep these questions in mind as you review the story of Matthew:
– What does this story show about this experience from Matthew's point of view, both in the classroom and with the bunny?
– What does it show us about how Matthew feels about himself?
– What does it show that Matthew knows how to do?

Matthew's story gives us a heart-filled example of the vital role living creatures and the natural world can play in the lives of children. Without this furry friend, Matthew might never have found any sanctuary from his stormy morning. He shows us his capacity for connection with the bunny that we cannot see in his interactions with people. In fact, the bunny gives him the experience of connection that the hectic classroom environment cannot provide.

Take Another Look

It is incumbent on us to offer children refuge from the hard, sterile, fast-paced, hectic world of modern society, institutional settings, urban environments, and commercial interests. It is their right and our utmost responsibility. Use the following activities to learn more about children in the natural world.

Observe Children in Natural Settings

Go to the beach, a park, the woods, or other outdoor place where children are playing. Choose three different children to observe, each in a different age range. Notice the details of how they make connections with the natural world. Use the following questions to guide your observations and some written reflections or discussion with your partner or group:

– What do you specifically see them do in relationship to the natural world?
– What seems to capture their interests?
– What seems to be fun and pleasurable?
– What questions do they seem to pursue?
– What are they trying to figure out about themselves and the natural world?

Observe Children with Animals or Other Living Creatures

Notice the way children connect with the pets or animals in your room. Keep a small notepad next to where the animal is and visit this location throughout the day when you see a child or children involved there. If you don't have a pet in your room, take your notepad outside with you each day and watch when children notice living creatures outdoors, for instance, birds, bugs, worms, and spiders. Take brief notes over a few weeks time. Use the following questions to guide your observations, reflective writing, or discussion with your partner or group:

– What do you specifically see them do in relationship to the animal or creature?
– What connections do they make with the animal or creature?
– What seems to capture their interests?
– What seems to be fun and pleasurable?
– What questions do they seem to pursue?
– What are they trying to figure out about themselves and the animal/creature?

Sample Observation: Grace Makes Art with Nature

Grace worked with natural building and design materials in the yard today. She gathered up all of the driftwood and arranged it to make a fort. She decorated the inside of her fort with pine branches, sticks, stones, and pinecones. She arranged these objects in beautiful ways by looking closely at their shapes, matching their curves and lines to create designs. She was very excited about her work and called to others, "Come on, you have to look at what I made."

More Things to Do

Besides watching children and their relationship to the natural world, it is important that you pursue this relationship yourself. This will give you further insight into how to plan this for children as well as more meaningful responses to their self-initiated explorations in nature.

Discover That No Two Things Are the Same

Working on your own or with a partner, find four sets of alike things from nature: two leaves from the same tree, two similar rocks, two of the same type of shell, two apples, or strawberries, for example. Look at each set for five minutes listing all of the ways they are different from each other.

Compose a "Dear Beautiful Butterfly" Letter

Write a dialogue between you and a favorite living creature, such as a bird, fish, dog, insect, lion, or butterfly. Think about what it would take to make friends with this creature. What would you have to do or say to be a part of its world? The goal of this activity is to challenge you to try out a different perspective from your own.

Try Another Perspective "Just for a Day"

Another way to try out a new perspective using animals is by exploring the children's book series *Just for a Day*. These books take you on a journey from the point of view of various animals. Excerpts from two of these books, *Catching the Wind* and *Lizard in the Sun,* are listed below. Study them and try to let them guide your imagination. Pick another creature and write your own version of *Just for a Day* with this insect or animal's perspective.

Catching the Wind

Imagine waking up one crisp morning and hearing the wind's voice calling you, changing you into a magnificent Canada goose. Imagine flying high in the windy sky as the world you know shrinks far below you. Come! Beat your powerful wings and soar over towns and fields—just for a day.

Lizard in the Sun

Imagine being touched by the sun as it slides into your shadowy room. Imagine growing smaller and smaller, changing your shape until you have four brown feet and a long brown tail. You are no longer a human. You are a tiny lizard called an American chameleon. Sometimes you are brown. Sometimes you are green. And always you are ready for adventure. Come! Be a lizard—just for a day.

Recommended Resources

Johnson, Stephen T. *City by Numbers.* New York: Viking, 1998. For those seeking beauty in the human-made world of urban settings, this book offers lovely photos to help you see shapes, textures, patterns, and colors in new ways.

Murphy, Pat, and William Neill. *By Nature's Design.* San Francisco: Chronicle Books, 1993. The beautiful text and photographs help our eyes discover the patterns that exist throughout nature. Included is a chapter on fractals, the approach scientists and mathematicians use to find order in natural structures. (Breathtaking fractal images are also available in calendars.)

Nabhan, Gary Paul, and Stephen Trimble. *The Geography of Childhood.* Boston: Beacon Press Books, 1994. This book defines why children need contact with the natural world and the "wild" for full development of their understanding of where we live. It is a sensitive examination of what a relationship to nature can mean for children and for all of us.

Rivkin, Mary S. *The Great Outdoors. Restoring Children's Right to Play Outside.* Washington, D.C.: NAEYC, 1995. This book sounds the call for schools and communities to restore children's outdoor play opportunities, gives inspiring examples of play spaces across the United States and the world, and offers practical ideas for bringing the great outdoors to your school.

Ryder, Joanne. *Catching the Wind.* New York: Mulberry Books, 1989. This story shows us how the world might look from the eye of a Canada goose.

————. *Lizard in the Sun.* New York: Mulberry Books, 1990. Filled with sensory words and images, this book gives us a taste of how a lizard might experience our world.

Stilgoe, John R. *Outside Lies Magic. Regaining History and Awareness in Everyday Places.* New York: Walker and Company, 1998. The author helps us notice the thousands of things that we often overlook. This book will help you become an explorer of the mysteries to be found in every corner.

Williams, Terry Tempest. *Desert Quartet.* New York: Pantheon Books, 1995. The author's detailed descriptions of the natural world help us understand what will be lost if we don't provide this for children.

7

STUDY SESSION

Observing How Children Seek Power, Drama, and Adventure

There was a child went forth every day,
And the first object he looked upon, that object he became,
And that object became part of him for the day or a certain part of the day,
Or for many years or stretching cycles of years.

Walt Whitman, *Leaves of Grass*

Learning Goals for This Study Session

In this study session you will

- Reconnect with the exhilaration of feeling adventurous, powerful, dramatic, and competent.
- Examine the significance of power, adventure, drama, and risk for children's development.
- Practice seeing the details of children's play involving power, adventure, drama, and challenge.

Reflect on the Quote

Walt Whitman reminds us that what children see around them has a tremendous impact on whom they become. Use these questions to spark your reflection on this topic.

– What are your reactions to this idea?
– What experiences from your own childhood confirm this?
– How do you see the children you work with being affected by what surrounds them?

Do some reflective writing or talk with a partner or a small group. You might want to use the teacher responses below to spark or extend your thinking.

> I am always amazed at how children use dramatic play to act out everything. They act out daddies, mommies and babies, kittens, bad guys and super heroes. I think they are doing this to understand the world around them. They seem to have to become something to understand it. I think that's what Walt Whitman means by this quote. —**Josie, preschool teacher**

> This quote really worries me. I see the children in my group, especially the boys, acting out all kinds of things they see in movies and on television. It is so violent. The latest rage is the new *Star Wars* movie. Even though we don't allow them to play with the guns or other weapons they bring to our program, they invent them. They call them lasers and spend a lot of time shooting each other and blowing things up. I worry that if what the quote says is true, then these children will "become" grown-ups who use violence to solve their problems. —**Carl, preschool teacher**

Art of Awareness Activity

Unmask Your Emotional Responses: As adults we've been taught to filter and restrict the emotional responses we have to situations around us. Both cultural values and our personal dispositions have influenced the mindsets we have developed about displaying our emotions. Children have a very different way of being in the world. Until they are schooled in another direction, their emotions are raw and unrestrained. They don't censor their reactions to experiences, but rather give full expression to how they are feeling.

Children use pretend play and drama as a way to understand and express the many feelings they experience. To remember what this exploration involves try the following activity.

1. Collect photos from a magazine or book that depict people's faces showing a variety of emotions.

2. As you look at each photo bring your emotional response to the forefront of your awareness. Try not to think about or analyze the photo; just let yourself feel your response.

3. As your feelings come to the surface, express them in a dramatic way. Use your body, facial expressions, and tone of voice. Express the feelings fully, with drama and flair.

4. If you do this alone, try looking in a mirror to see your own expressions. Working with a partner or small group, do it as a performance for each other.

5. Try this several times so you become more comfortable with feeling your emotions and acting them out.

Learn to See Childhood As a World of Exhilarating and Scary Adventures

Children are small and the world is so big. On the one hand, they are eager to explore and try everything. On the other hand, children are often beset with fears and hesitations. In the context of normal development, most children successfully wrestle with their fears and develop a sense of competency. Even when they have experienced childhood trauma, most children are resilient, and with ample support, can overcome an inclination toward fear, self-blame, or unhealthy coping mechanisms.

Sample Observation: I Superman

Parr, the youngest and smallest child in the class of three to five year olds, has been wearing his Superman pajamas to preschool each day. "I'm Superman," he announces as he jumps from the climber, builds with blocks, plays with playdough, and paints with watercolors.

Sample Observation: Hot Lava

Natalie spent the morning painting multiple pictures of volcanoes at the painting easel today. As she painted the hot lava coming out of her volcanoes she made loud blasting sounds to represent the explosions.

There are many real things to fear in the world, and our particular culture often uses stories of violence as a form of entertainment and commercial interests. There is ample evidence that this is both appealing to and negatively impacting children. Gaining a sense of power can easily become equated with violence. For young children, the distinction between violence with real consequences and the violence of a TV show or video game becomes blurred.

Children's play often appears to have elements of TV shows or video games. They imitate the sounds of guns, bombs, and destruction and often lend their full bodies to a portrayal of explosions. This is understandably alarming to adults. But rather than immediately responding with rules or threatening consequences, we need to do some research to uncover the emotional elements of why this play is appealing to children rather than frightening to them. When we observe closely and try to understand a young child's perspective in this play, we can see it in the context of their social-emotional developmental themes. These include

- Acting powerful to overcome fears and feel competent
- Trying out risks and challenges to develop self-esteem, confidence, and competence
- Creating drama and adventure to try to understand the world around them
- Expressing their ideas and powerful feelings about the world

In our adult lives we may continue to work on our social-emotional themes through creating drama in our families and circle of friends. Or we may immerse ourselves in theater or literature to keep exploring these themes. Some of us find counseling or a spiritual group useful. Whatever our avenues to work on these issues as adults, we need to remember that children, too, need avenues for their developmental process. Recalling our own childhood experiences with drama and adventure will help us recognize this and remind us to provide those opportunities for the children in our programs. The goal is to offer experiences for children to create and invent their own explorations of power, rather than consume and mimic what the media feeds them.

Practice Remembering Your Childhood Drama and Adventure

Recall some of your vivid childhood dramas and adventures. Use these questions to pull out the details of your memories.

– Where did you play and act these out?
– Who was involved?
– What props did you use?
– Where did your ideas for these experiences come from? Were they related to events in your family life or community, or tied to things you heard about the world, books you read, TV shows, or movies you saw?
– Try to recall the feelings you had when you acted out these themes. Did you feel frightened, helpless, competent, or powerful in your adventures?

Share your stories with a partner or small group, considering the following questions. If you're working alone, you might try writing on the topics suggested by the questions.

– Were your experiences similar or different from others? Was your experience more typical or unusual?
– What value and importance did these experiences have in your life, both then and now?
– How do your experiences compare with those of children today?

Observation Practice

As you consider the times you felt most powerful in your childhood, reflect on how often this was related to being daring and adventurous. Most of us have favorite childhood memories of play that the grown-ups would have stopped if they had known about it. Try to keep your experiences in mind as you read some observation stories of children involved in drama, challenge, and adventure.

Bad Guys on the Playground

"Are the bad guys out there yet?" Nate excitedly calls out to Adam from the snack table. With this question John, Lucinda, and Nate jump up to the window to look out to the playground with Adam. "Yeah! There they are!" Lucinda declares.

The preschoolers hurriedly clean up their snack area and get on their shoes and coats to head outside. This same scene has been happening for a few weeks now. The preschoolers anticipate outdoor time with excitement and trepidation. The "bad guys" are three of the kindergarteners who join this group in the play yard for recess each day. They are bigger and older, and these three and four year olds notice and respect these differences.

Once on the play yard, the chase game begins. Nate bravely runs up to the three boys and shouts and laughs, "You can't catch me." The boys begin to chase him until he scampers to the top of the climber, the "safe zone." His comrades are up there waiting. The kindergartners look up menacingly, but respect the rules of the game.

John asks worriedly, "Did they get you?" Nate says breathlessly, "No, I runned faster and I climbed so fast to here." Lucinda brags, "Yeah, they can't get me too." John says, "Come on, let's go! They'll never get us."

They run out to the center of the grassy area, taunting the "bad guys," fiercely growling, with eyes bright and alert. The bad guys take the bait, and the chase begins again. The preschoolers' movements are quick as they dodge their pursuers.

At one point Adam runs to a teacher and clings to her side, hiding from the kindergartner at his tail. The teacher asks him, "Are you done playing this chase game, Adam? You can tell Suki if you'd like to stop." Adam looks out from behind the teacher, growls at Suki, darts to the climber, and bounds to the top. Safe again.

The game ends for today as the kindergartners are called back to their room. It will in all likelihood begin again tomorrow as it has now for weeks and even years past. When the "bad guys" were preschoolers last year they played similar games, only they called their foe the "big kids."

Reflect on your own or work with a partner or group to find the meaning of this observation story. Use these observation questions to guide your thinking:

- What do you think the preschool children are pursuing through this "bad guy" drama? What do they say about themselves and the "bad guys" that gives you clues to the meaning of this play for them?
- What do their physical actions tell you about their abilities and the importance of this play to them?
- In what ways are the kindergarten children playing differently from the preschoolers?
- What do you think the kindergartners' point of view about this play might be?
- What are the kindergartners gaining from this game?

In the play-yard scene above, each of the children seemed clear about their roles and confident that they could handle the drama that would unfold. In fact, they need this self-designed drama to unfold to reassure them that they are self-sufficient and able to handle adversity. What could be more important for young children facing a powerful, unpredictable world?

Notice how these children invented their own scripts for the familiar "bad guys" drama. They were drawing on internal resources, not acting out a part invented by Hollywood. This story showed preschoolers and kindergartners playing together. The opportunity to play outdoors in a mixed-age setting is good for both the younger and older children. The preschoolers shared these experiences:

- Excitement in anticipating the bad guys and the chase; looking forward to it, even though they feel some anxious concern
- Competence in their physical abilities, their abilities to run and climb
- Willingness to continue the risk of going back to the chase
- Certainty they can keep themselves safe with the rules, "the safe zone," their teacher, and friends

There are fewer details of the kindergartners' perspective in this story, but we do learn that they played the same game when they were preschoolers. They obviously enjoyed it and can now continue playing from the vantage point of being older. The kindergartners shared these experiences:

- Responsibility to take their role as big kids seriously, having seen it modeled the year before when they were preschoolers
- Empathy for their preschool friends, with eagerness to challenge them to take up the exhilaration of the chase and find their power
- Recognition that they are older and have worked through their fears
- The experience of their own competence and abilities

In this drama the teacher's response could have been to take charge and try to stop the game. Instead, we see her understanding the excitement of feeling scared and powerful, while reassuring the children that she is watching the scene and looking out for them when she asks, "Do you really want to play this?" She pays close attention. If the game did erupt into a conflict that nobody wanted, she would step in. This is a tricky role for a teacher to play, one requiring knowledge of the individual children and the meaning of the game. Having mastered observation skills and knowledge of child development, you can stay tuned to the underlying meaning of action games and help them stay challenging, but fun and safe.

In years past, like those of the memories we revisited in the last chapter, kids got to play outside without constant grown-up supervision. They learned to work through these issues with each other. Though we can't leave children unsupervised in our programs today, we need to provide for and protect this kind of adventure play. If children don't get to experiment with power and adventure when they are young, they will likely pursue more dangerous avenues in search of these experiences as adolescents.

A Balancing Act

The teachers in the toddler room have put out some large motor equipment for the children to climb and play on. Eighteen-month-old Delmar is drawn to the large, soft wedge-shaped ramp that is in the middle of the carpet. He waddles up to the lowest edge, steps on, and cautiously walks up to the higher end. As he tries to turn himself around at the top, he falls over and off the ramp. His first look is one of alarm, but then, realizing he's okay, he laughs, gets up, runs back to the lower end, and proceeds to climb up the wedge again.

This time Delmar successfully negotiates the turn at the top without falling. He squeals and barrels down the ramp. Tripping over his own feet, he falls forward, smacking his face into the wedge. He sits up and begins to wail. The teacher, who has been standing nearby supervising, quickly moves over to comfort him. He continues to cry for about thirty seconds and then gets up and walks slowly to the top of the wedge again. He turns, and at a much slower speed, walks successfully down the ramp. Laughing uproariously at the bottom, Delmar turns immediately and runs back to the top, falling over halfway up, popping up again, and making it to the top. He turns and goes down the ramp again, this time a bit faster, squealing with delight as he runs.

Delmar does this same toddler activity over and over again, going faster each time and even falling on his face a number of times. Rather than crying when he falls, these face plants become a part of his game as he laughs and gets up to do it again.

Use the following questions to guide you as you reflect on the meaning of this observation:

– What do Delmar's actions tell us about what he is working on?
– What can we tell about his disposition toward learning from his change in moods?
– What strategies do we see him use to overcome the difficulties?

When a child like Delmar takes on the challenges of speed and coordination, he is both exhilarated and somewhat cautious. As we watch his adventure, our adult urge is usually to issue additional cautions, "Be careful," "Slow down or you'll get hurt." For a moment our fears seem justified as he falls and bursts into tears. But wait; take another look. Delmar seems undaunted and, in fact, all the more challenged to try his climb again. Consider the benefits he gets from this pursuit as compared to reminders that he might get hurt.

Our foremost job as teachers is to keep children safe, but safety should not be equated with the absence of any risk. What would happen if Delmar could not pursue this challenge? How might he come to see himself and his abilities?

Take Another Look

Do you keep an eye out for ways in which children experiment with having power? Do you listen and watch carefully and wait before intervening in play dramas involving power? Do you keep your eyes and ears open for examples of how children view power, where it comes from, and what they can do with it? When you watch attentively, you can learn so much more about this important aspect of childhood!

Sample Observation: Rock Power

Rachel's discovery of a large rock on the playground led to many opportunities to feel strong and powerful. She carried the rock to a tub, dropped it in, and began pushing the tub all over the playground.

Observe Children's Play Involving Power and Adventure

Spend some time observing children involved in an adventure or exploration of power. Notice the themes of their play and the props they use to act out their dramas. Can you determine what may be influencing them and the underlying issues they are trying to work out through the play?

Observe Children Negotiating Risk

Observe three different children on a playground or another setting where they are able to challenge themselves physically. Collect the details of how each of them approaches risk taking. What is the perspective and ability of each child? What are they trying to understand and work through in their play? Are there any cultural influences you can identify? Notice your own response to any risky or daring behavior the children try.

More Things to Do

As you strive to become more comfortable with children's risk taking and action dramas, it will be useful to explore more of your own relationship to risk taking. Dispositions toward risk are different for each of us. Our own tolerance and safety thresholds need to be acknowledged.

Assess Your Own Response to Risk Taking

Look at the photos below and notice your immediate reaction. Are you alarmed, disturbed, fascinated, or delighted by what the children are doing?

If you were to place yourself on this continuum of possible responses, where would we find you?

That's not safe! Someone's going to get hurt. I'm going to close the block area.	You know better than that. You know our rule. You can't build higher than your shoulders.	You are really figuring out how to build as high as possible! How can we be sure that you and the blocks are stable and no one will get hurt?	Wow, that's such a high tower! Do you think you can balance one of the wooden trucks up there?

Do some reflective writing or talk with others about the following questions:

- What is influencing the first response you have to this scene?
- Do you feel there is any real danger for the children in this picture?
- What self-concept and identity are children developing for themselves in activities such as this?
- Are you satisfied with your initial reaction to this situation, or would you hope to respond in a different way?
- As an observer of this play, what is important to pay attention to?

Study Emotional Expressions

To continue heightening your awareness of the different ways people express emotions, try this activity throughout the course of a day. Choose an adult and child to closely watch and pretend you are their understudy, preparing yourself to portray them in an upcoming drama. Pay close attention to their body language, facial expressions, tones of voice, and other ways they express ideas and feelings. If appropriate, take photographs that you can study.

Practice standing in front of a mirror and portraying each of the people you studied. Do some reflective writing or discuss the details and discoveries of your day with a partner or small group.

Recommended Resources

Gallas, Karen. *Sometimes I Can Be Anything. Power, Gender and Identity in a Primary Classroom.* New York: Teachers College Press, 1998. This teacher-researcher-author tells fascinating stories of how the boys and girls in her class use different behaviors to gain power and recognition and how gender dynamics become intertwined with issues of race, culture, status, and belonging.

Goleman, Daniel. *Emotional Intelligence.* New York: Bantam, 1997. The author suggests that our current view of intelligence is more limited than is useful in understanding and educating children.

Hannaford, Carla. *Smart Moves. Why Learning Is Not All in Your Head.* Atlanta: Great Ocean Publishers, 1995. Written by a neurophysiologist and educator, this book describes how large body movement activity is related to children's emotional as well as cognitive and physical development.

Levin, Diane E. *Remote Control Childhood.* Washington, D.C.: NAEYC, 1998. A chilling look at how electronic media with all its association of violence with power is shaping the lives of young children. Includes useful guidelines for taking action with children, corporations, and policymakers.

Lieberman, Alicia F. *The Emotional Life of the Toddler.* New York: Free Press, 1995. With many examples of the ways toddlers are learning from reactions to their emotional expressions, this book offers insight into the meaning of much of this observed behavior.

Paley, Vivian Gussin. *Bad Guys Don't Have Birthdays. Fantasy Play at Four.* Chicago: The University of Chicago Press, 1988. This is a thoroughly engaging book recalling a group of children's fantasy play. Paley is masterful at telling the detailed stories of children's play and offering profound and useful insights and analysis.

———. *Boys and Girls. Superheroes in the Doll Corner.* Chicago: The University of Chicago Press, 1984. This teacher-author describes the differences in the ways boys and girls play in kindergarten. The children's conversations, stories, and dramas are interwoven with Paley's observations and insightful analysis.

8

STUDY SESSION

Observing Children's Eagerness toward Representation and Literacy

Every child has a story to tell, and within that story is the secret to reaching her or him as a learner. Children's stories are windows into their uniqueness and clues on how to connect the child and the curriculum.

Herb Kohl

Learning Goals for This Study Session

In this study session you will

- Practice using a writing web to experience the satisfaction of creative expression.
- Recall memories of your own "storytelling" as a child.
- Examine meaningful experiences where children develop representational and literacy skills.
- Practice observing the details of children's efforts to represent their ideas and experiences.

Reflect on the Quote

Reflect on the words of Herb Kohl regarding children's stories. Use the following questions to guide your thinking:

– What do you think Herb Kohl means by the concept of children having stories to tell?
– How do you think this relates to observing children?

Do some reflective writing or discuss this with others. Consider this teacher's reflection along with your own.

> As I've been learning to observe children, I am beginning to see that everything they do shows me the "story" about what they are thinking and feeling. I feel like I have really changed how I think about them. I used to think they were cute and fun to be with. Now I think of them as amazing, complicated people, full of curiosity and adventure. I guess you might say being with them is like reading a good book or story. I can't wait to see what will happen next. —**Aida, preschool teacher**

Art of Awareness Activity

Write the Natural Way: In *Writing the Natural Way*, Gabriele Lusser Rico describes a creative writing process she designed from observing the natural writing and story-telling strategies of young children. Her observations of children led her to believe that children bring an attitude of wonder and openness toward creative expression and are eager to dictate and write elaborate stories at a young age. She states that the ways we are taught to read and write in school inhibit our natural urge for self-expression because of the emphasis on rules and standards. The techniques she details in her book are designed to release creative potential and to trigger language capabilities from the right hemisphere of the brain. They involve clustering and webbing activities to call on the creative storytelling side of the brain before trying to use rules and conventions of writing to construct a product.

Rico makes the case that these are two very distinct aspects of writing. When we are forced to focus only on the conventions of writing, we lose the joy and motivation to express ourselves in writing. Try this webbing activity adapted from her book to stretch your creativity and experience the natural source of pleasure and gratification that writing can offer you. It will also help you begin to notice the beauty in the details of what is around you all of the time.

1. Choose something in nature as the focus of your observation.
2. Draw a circle in the middle of a piece of paper. Write a word for what you are observing in the middle of the circle.

3. Look closely at the object or animal, noticing the sensory details: color, texture, light, sounds, how your body feels, and what is on your mind as you look.

4. Brainstorm words to describe the details you're noticing. Put each new word or phrase in a circle connected to the central circle with a line. Your paper will start to look like a spiderweb. Look at the examples below if this is confusing. Think of as many descriptive words as you can, and add them to the web.

5. Use the words on this web to begin to formulate some sentences about your experience.

Here are some examples of how teachers have created webs and turned them into stories. Beginning with something alive, other than a child, is a good place to start. It frees you from the concern about "getting it right."

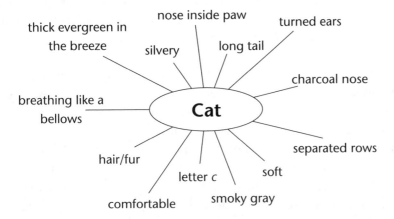

The smoky silver-gray cat is sleeping soundly, charcoal nose tucked neatly inside a tightly curled paw. Slow rhythmic breathing gives the illusion that he's an old bellows fanning the blacksmith's hot coals. The curve of his back forms a perfect letter C that ends with the pointed tip of his long tail curled gently around his hind leg. His ears are tweaked clockwise to his head. His fur separates in rows of varying lengths as the bellows inside him fills with air and gently expels. The uneven rows remind me of an evergreen tree blowing in the breeze. He looks very comfortable. I think I'll let him sleep. —**Kathy**

Then my son got his high-powered telescope out and focused it on the moon. It was the first time I had really seen the moon. The moon, whiter than the purest newly fallen snow, glistens, crystal cold in the clear dark night sky.

Mountains with jagged peaks appear. Close by, a huge crater lies reminding me of the splash made by cereal when it is poured in white milk. Thousands of smaller craters cover the cold, milky white surface of the moon making pock marks. —**Gail, student teacher**

Learn to See Childhood As a Time to Construct Meaning

When provided with open-ended materials, time, and support, young children eagerly create representations of their ideas and experiences. When we observe closely, we can see that these are more than creative outlets. Representational experiences are central to children's learning processes. They help children make meaning out of a variety of social and cognitive code systems that shape their world.

Children are typically less inhibited than adults to openly "play with understandings" as they build, take on pretend roles, draw, paint, and use any object within their reach to show what is on their minds. These initial expressions of symbolic thinking help them organize their understanding of the world and lay the foundation for working with other symbolic languages such as print, math concepts, and computer programming. These opportunities strengthen the parts of their brain that allow them to communicate in and interpret a wide range of representations, including written and spoken languages, music, dance, science, poetry, and literature.

In our efforts to "get children ready for school" we often reduce or trivialize children's opportunities for creative representation by giving them such projects as making bunnies from paper plates. This limits their creativity and sense of possibility. When the goal for a project is to learn to follow directions and copy a model, children aren't gaining experience with using images for their own thinking and communicating with others—and yet this latter experience is crucial for early literacy.

A similar process occurs when we reduce the idea of learning to read and write to memorizing and copying letters. The sense of power and expansiveness that comes from reading and writing eludes children who are only taught through prescribed, out-of-context literacy activities. In contrast, children who are surrounded with meaningful print and stories can't wait to unlock the secrets of this powerful form of human communication.

When we carefully study their activities, both the processes and products, we begin to discover children's unique expressiveness and their remarkable abilities to create form and structure out of the complex and often confusing world they live in. We see their eagerness to learn to use the tools and skills that will help them make their questions, thinking, and feelings visible. As Herb Kohl reminds us, when we watch closely we can see the amazing "stories" children are telling us about themselves.

Children's "readiness to learn" comes from their natural curiosity about the world and the urge to make sense of it through creative, investigative representations. We must counter the pressures to narrowly define learning to read and write and give children significant recognition for their explorations in all modes of representation. To help them enrich and grow confident in these basics of literacy development, we must first notice and respect the various forms of "stories" children bring to us.

Practice Remembering Your Own "Storytelling"

Think back to your own childhood and the way you used representation to express yourself and make sense of the world. Describe the forms you used and some specific details about what you did. Consider the categories of representation listed below as you search your memory bank.

- **Pretend play:** What props did you use? What were the themes and stories of your dramas?
- **Drawing or painting:** What tools and materials did you use? What do you remember sketching or painting pictures of?
- **Building and construction:** What tools and materials did you use? What constructions did you make?

Reflecting on some of these memories, how do you think these experiences impact how you see yourself as a thinker today? Do you think of yourself as creative and quick to express your ideas with a variety of materials? Do you enjoy these expressions of others, in literature, the arts, music, dance, textiles, or architecture, for example?

How can you relate your experiences to the children you work with? It is also useful to remember specific experiences you had with learning to read or write.

- What do you remember about how you learned to read and write?
- What were the positive and negative aspects of the learning process?
- Did you grow up thinking of reading and writing as a necessary task or something you enjoy and are eager to do whenever you have the opportunity?
- If your home language was not English, how was that addressed when you were learning to read and write? How did you feel about the way your two languages were handled at school?

Observation Practice

The following photos and notes were taken by preschool teacher Veronica as she worked to uncover the children's interest in and strategies for telling stories.

Sample Observations: Exploring Danger and Safety

"The fireworks come out of the top. The people sit all around the bottom. There is a place for the ambulance in case anyone gets hurt. I call it the JFXYZR Biggo Fireworks Machine." —**Jeffrey (7)**

"We are in our house. Look, my mom and dad are shrinking. See, they are getting really small. The big one is me. See the little lines coming out of their heads? They are yelling to me, Rich, Rich, help us!" —**Rich (5)**

"This is my grandma in a rocking chair. See inside, that baby is me. My grandma is rocking me." —**Kira (4)**

"This is a volcano. It has hot lava shooting out of it. This is me climbing up the volcano. I am wearing a helmet because the volcano is really mad. My helmet has antennae on it so the volcano will think I'm a bug." —**Ben (5)**

Study the children's work and reflect on your own or discuss these questions with a partner or small group.

– What do you notice about how the children used art materials? Consider the use of shade, line, shape, and form. What representations have they made?
– Compare what they have made to what they have said about their representations. What does the work show that the children are exploring or understanding?
– What skills and knowledge does this work show us that each child has?

When you study each of these representations carefully, you not only notice the imaginative and skillful ways the children represented their ideas, you also see the underlying developmental themes they are exploring. These "stories" show children wrestling with their fears and the powerful and magical things they notice about the world. Each of the representations here provides windows into how the individual children are addressing their fears and their need to feel powerful. Kira has created a three-dimensional model of comfort. Ben and Rich have made their fears visible and therefore manageable through their work. Jeffrey has created a powerful machine. These symbolic representations have important meaning and learning for the children and enable the children as well as the adults to understand better what they are working on cognitively and emotionally.

Lost Dog

"The dog is lost," Cory announces as she climbs down from the loft where she has been looking for one of the stuffed animals that has been a big part of the children's puppy and kitty play. The entire group rallies for a search throughout the classroom.

"She's not in the block bin or the spaceship," Sam calls out to the others. "We better make a sign," Cory says seriously. "It should say, 'Lost Dog.'" The three to five year olds rush to get markers and paper off the shelf in the drama area and begin making signs.

"How do you spell lost dog?" LaToya asks. The teacher writes the words on a piece of paper and the children earnestly copy them onto their drawings of dogs. "We need to put these where people can see them, so they know we have a lost dog," Cory plans.

Someone calls out, "Get the tape." The children eagerly rush around the room finding places on the doors, walls, and windows to tape their signs. As parents begin arriving for pickup time the children excitedly show them their work.

"We have a lost dog," Cory tells her mom. "I read that on your sign," her mom says, smiling. "Someone will find that dog for sure, 'cause they'll see the sign," Cory says proudly as she leaves for the day.

Reflect on this story by yourself or with a partner or small group. Use the following questions to spark your thinking:

– What are these children exploring and thinking about in this play?
– What do the children show us they know about reading and writing?

– How are they using what they know in their play?
– How do the environment and the teacher support their expression?

Symbolic representation comes in many forms. Pretend play and drawing are a large part of the symbolic thinking that children use in their early childhood. If they are surrounded with a print-rich environment where literacy is used in meaningful ways and is about "real life" events and activities, then children come to understand its power and purpose quickly. We can see this so clearly in the story of the lost dog. Children are eager to know about and use these magical symbols. They show us this in all of the ways they pretend to write in their play and in their practice attempts at reading and writing.

Look What I Understand

After spending time outside by the climber where there were jump ropes, Johnny went inside to get paper and the box of markers. He came back out, sat down at the picnic table under the tree, and carefully smoothed out his paper. Sorting through the markers, he pulled out a black one and began writing letters across his paper, going from left to right.

He called out the names of letters, "X A N," saying them several times as he continued to form different letters on his paper. B R K B A and so on.

As he got to the right side of the paper he started a new line beginning back near the left side of the paper. Reaching the end of this row, he went back to the left side again and made a third row, no longer calling out letter names but showing great concentration on his face. Then he drew two horizontal lines across the paper from left to right, one under the first row of his letters and one under the second.

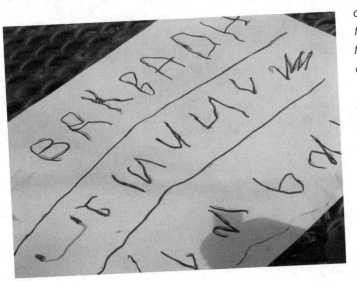

Johnny began going through the marker box again, accurately naming colors as he picked them up. "Red. Black," he said, and then, smelling the next marker, he said, "Grape. This one's grape."

He used these markers to make hooplike marks on the top left-hand corner of his paper, one inside the other, like a rainbow. Then to the left of the second line of letters he put two black dots a few inches apart. He carefully chose another marker and made an orange loop connecting the two dots. "That's my long jump rope. For my school."

Johnny then jumped up and ran to his teacher, Cindy, saying, "Teacher, look. Look."

"That's great, Johnny. You made a sign with so many words on it. What do all those words say?"

"All that spells jump rope."

"Oh. Like our jump rope over there. How should we put this sign up?"

"No. I want it inside in the mailbox." And off he went to put it there.

Johnny soon returned with a stack of more white paper. Again, he carefully placed one in front of him, smoothed it out, chose a marker, and immediately drew three horizontal lines from left to right, spaced fairly evenly down the page.

He smoothed out his paper again, exchanged the marker for a different one, and began to write distinctly separate letters, starting at the left side of the page and carefully bringing each one down to rest on the line. After each letter he lifted his marker and left some space before starting to make the next. He worked his way across the paper this way, and when he got to the right side he exchanged markers again and with a black one pressed hard and scribbled a mark at the end of the line. "That's out," he said, repeating it again and pointing with his marker, "That is out."

He started a second line in a new color, making a careful purple A, then a turquoise B, and then a two-colored H, drawing a pink line, then a yellow line. On the next line he made other multicolored letters, still moving across the page from left to right. "My brother has his own room, " he announced. And with that he picked up his paper and headed inside again, saying, "This is my brother."

Reflect on this story by yourself, with a partner, or with a small group. Use these questions to guide your reflections:

- What understandings do you think this child is exploring and expressing?
- What does he show us he knows about reading and writing?
- What guesses do you have about where his ideas came from? What else do you need to find out?
- How do the environment and the teacher support his representational efforts?

Many classrooms have a reading corner and writing area, but often teachers restrict the materials in them for use only in that area. What opportunities are missed when we isolate literacy activities in this way? What would have been lost for this child if he hadn't had the freedom to go inside and get the pens and markers he wanted to use outside? What if there hadn't been a space for him to sit and do this representational work?

Think of all the places we typically have reading and writing materials in our homes. When children see all the places and ways in which reading and writing are useful, they will naturally want to express themselves in this way, as is so clearly evident in this story of Johnny.

How can the many routines of reading and writing in the adult world be made more visible for the children to become involved within your program? Watch for examples of how children want to express themselves in writing when you model and narrate the purpose of print.

Take Another Look

If you watch for them, you will see children using representations in meaningful ways all of the time. Try some of the following activities in your own setting to strengthen your commitment to provide for these opportunities.

Examine and Enrich Your Environment to Support Literacy

Examine your learning environment, indoor and outdoors, to see where more reading and writing materials can be added to encourage the children to play

with literacy. Beyond a reading or writing corner, do you have books and writing materials in most areas of your room? Are they available for use outside? Many early childhood resource books have lists of props that can be put into the environment to encourage children to incorporate various forms of early literacy into their play. For instance, see *Much More than the ABCs* by Judith Schickedanz (Washington D.C.: NAEYC, 1999). The point here is to help children use beginning reading and writing in their daily activities. In addition, we want to expose them to other ways adults use literacy for work routines, reference, and for enjoyment.

Observe Literacy Play

Once you have the props in place observe the children's use of them in their play. Ask yourself these questions to deepen your observations:

– How are the children using the materials?
– What are the contexts in which the children use them?
– What do the children seem to understand about literacy and how to use it?
– What are the children's attitudes toward literacy? How can you tell?

Examine Your Environment and Enrich It with Other Representational Materials

In addition to literacy materials, what other kinds of representational materials are available for children to use in exploring and expressing their ideas? Here are some questions to ask yourself as you assess your environment:

– Does the dress-up or dramatic play area have props that are more open-ended than just the traditional housekeeping or topical themes like doctor's office and supermarket?
– Have you considered the option of more open-ended materials that would allow for any of these themes to be represented by the children as they create their own props?
– What kinds of open-ended building and construction materials are available?
– Have you enriched the traditional areas for blocks and Lego plastic building blocks with things like a variety of rocks, driftwood, sturdy cardboard tubes, ramps, gutters, carpet and fabric scraps, masking tape on dispensers, and wire?
– Is there an art area or studio with a variety of everyday representational materials available?
– Do you have a range of scrap materials, colors of paper, markers, and different kinds of paints?
– Are there numerous ways for children to attach things together such as glue, tape, and wire?

To observe children telling the stories about their ideas, you will need to enrich your environment with representational materials.

Study Children's Work

Using these questions, study a variety of children's creative representations: drawings, paintings, constructions, sculptures, and pretend play scenes.

– What do you notice about the materials the children use and how they use them? Notice the use of color, line, shape and form, design, and story.
– What representations have they made?
– Compare what they have made to what they have said about their work. What does the work show that each of the children are exploring or understanding?
– What skills and knowledge does this work reveal?

Study Self-Portraits and Name Writing

Literacy specialist Evelyn Lieberman suggests that preschool teachers periodically ask children to draw a picture of themselves and write their names, starting at the very beginning of children's time in their classrooms. If the children say they can't write, you could suggest that they just pretend to write their name. Keep a collection of these samples to study what the children in your group know about representational drawing and writing. Ask yourself questions such as these:

– Do the children show they understand the difference between writing and drawing?
– Do they pretend to write by making lines or scribbles?
– Do they make marks for separate words or use one long cursivelike line?
– Do they know how to make some of the letters of their name?
– How do they place the letters of their name—in order or randomly?

You can tell a lot about what children know about writing by comparing your analysis with resources on the developmental stages of writing, such as the Schickeldanz book cited earlier.

More Things to Do

The more we do to explore our own understandings of the representational and decoding process to communicate, the better we can support these processes with children. Try these activities to gain more experience with the representational process.

Practice Other Forms of Representation

Outside of basic writing and reading for information, many of us haven't developed our representational skills. In fact, our lack of support for this development has left many of us feeling we aren't creative, and we are intimidated when asked to work with art materials, play music, or read dramatically. Invest some time exploring various materials such as watercolors, clay, and wire, and other forms of expressing ideas such as rap, haiku poems, and improvisational theater activities. Take a workshop or class on these expressive arts as part of your professional development to deepen your understanding about supporting children's efforts.

Experiment with Decoding Symbolic Representations

Use this activity to gain more insight into how children learn to decode abstract symbols. From your public library or the Internet gather some of the following items for you and your partner or group to examine: X rays, examples of Braille, Egyptian hieroglyphics, cave drawings, samples of Japanese calligraphy, pictures of sign language, Morse code, diagrams of technology, or satellite photography.

Work together to decode the meaning or "story" of each discussing these questions:

– What clues helped you decipher the meaning of this story?
– If you were to tell it as a story, what would you say about this?
– What could you do to further explore your hunches about the meaning?
– How does this activity give you insight into your work with children?

Explore Representing to Learn

College instructor Tom Drummond developed an earlier version of this activity to explore how we learn in collaboration with others and by representing our theories in drawings. Collect a variety of objects that have some hidden moveable parts as part of their function, things like a kitchen timer, a pen with a variety of ink colors, wind-up toys, a combination lock, an Etch-a-Sketch drawing toy, kaleidoscope, or staple gun. Work with a partner or a small group and choose one of the objects to examine. Follow this procedure in exploring your object:

1. Look at the object closely, exploring and noticing all of the mechanisms and features that make it work. At first, try to do this without talking. Do not take the item apart.

2. Share your ideas with one another about how you think the object works. Try demonstrating to one another by manipulating the object or using your body to show your ideas.

3. Take a few minutes for each of you to sketch your theory of how the object works. You can use other materials to make it two- or three-dimensional if that helps.

4. Share your drawings with one another and see if any of your theories change or get supported.

5. Discuss how each of the forms of representation (discussion, demonstration, and drawing) assisted with your learning about the object.

6. Discuss the role that other people played in helping you understand. What else would have been helpful?

7. Talk about how this experience relates to children's use of representation for learning and what they need from teachers.

Recommended Resources

Ashton-Warner, Sylvia. *Teacher.* New York: Simon & Schuster, 1963. A ground-breaking account of the author's work using her observations of children and their culture to teach them to read and write.

Cadwell, Louise. *Bringing Reggio Emilia Home.* New York: Teachers College Press, 1997. Along with the story of creating a school with inspiration from Reggio Emilia, this book offers practical examples of observing and analyzing children's drawings along with their transcribed conversations.

Clemens, Sydney Gurewitz. *The Sun's Not Broken, A Cloud's Just in the Way.* Mt. Rainier, Washington: Gryphon House, 1983. A moving account of how the author drew inspiration from the work of Sylvia Ashton-Warner for her work in an urban preschool program.

Davidson, J. I. *Emergent Literacy and Dramatic Play in Early Education.* Albany, NY: Delmar, 1996. The author describes how to facilitate language and literacy-rich play with many specific examples.

Engel, Brenda. *Considering Children's Art. Why and How to Value Their Works.* Washington, D.C.: NAEYC, 1995. The author offers perspectives on observing children's art as well as a clear description of how art contributes to learning in many subject areas.

Gallas, Karen. *The Languages of Learning. How Children Talk, Write, Dance, Draw and Sing Their Understanding of the World.* New York: Teachers College Press, 1994. The teacher-author demonstrates through specific stories of her classroom how young children communicate their knowledge of the world through a wide range of representations. She presents a compelling case for how the arts can transform the curriculum.

Hall, Nigel, and Anne Robinson. *Exploring Writing and Play in the Early Years.* London: David Fulton Publishers, 1998. With a variety of specific examples and illustrations the authors show the close relationship between children's socio-dramatic play and exploration of a wide range of uses of writing.

Hucko, Bruce. *A Rainbow at Night. The World in Words and Pictures by Navajo Children.* San Francisco: Chronicle Books, 1996. The author has been called a "children's art coach," and the text, photos, and artwork of the children give us a vivid picture of how children use symbols and designs to communicate what they understand. There are related exercises to explore your own understandings of what you see the children investigating with their art.

———. *Where There Is No Name for Art.* Santa Fe, New Mexico: School of American Research Press, 1996. The children's art and descriptions of its meaning are a terrific example of the relationship between culture and forms of symbolic representation.

Jones, Elizabeth, and Gretchen Reynolds. *The Play's the Thing. Teachers' Roles in Children's Play.* New York: Teachers College Press, 1996. This is a very readable, engaging set of observations and examples of how teachers can support children's play and representational experiences.

Paley, Vivian. *The Boy Who Would Be a Helicopter.* Cambridge, Massachusetts: Harvard University Press, 1990. This engaging book is centered on the story of a child who uses dramatic play to become part of the group.

Reynolds, Gretchen, and Elizabeth Jones. *Master Players. Learning From Children at Play.* New York: Teachers College Press, 1997. A companion text to their earlier title with detailed descriptions of the complexity involved in children's everyday play and the way that supports their learning.

Rico, Gabriele Lusser. *Writing the Natural Way.* New York: J. P. Tarcher Inc, 1983. The author draws on her observations of children learning to write to develop theories and strategies for adults to gain confidence in their writing.

9

STUDY SESSION

Observing How Children Form Relationships and Negotiate Conflict

A flower is relatively small. Everyone has many associations with a flower, the idea of flowers. You put out your hand to touch the flower and lean forward to smell it, maybe touch it with your lips almost without thinking, or give it to someone to please them. Still, in a way, nobody sees a flower really, it is so small, we haven't time. And to see takes time like to have a friend takes time.

Georgia O'Keeffe

Learning Goals for This Study Session

In this study session you will

- Practice looking attentively using contour drawings.
- Recall important relationships from your childhood.
- Relish the warmth and kindness that children bring to relationships.
- Examine what you learned about conflict in your childhood.
- Practice seeing relationships and conflict from children's perspectives.

Reflect on the Quote

Georgia O'Keeffe reminds us of the importance of time in making connections and seeing the world. Use these questions to guide your reflections on her words:

- What does this quote mean to you?
- Does it remind you of any recent experiences?
- How does this quote relate to your work with children?

Do some reflective writing and talk with another person or a group about your thinking. You might want to use the teacher responses below to spark or extend your thinking.

I feel that this quote relates to seeing things only on the surface. Most people don't notice the beauty in the world. We are in such a hurry to get from place to place that we forget the simple pleasures of hearing birds singing or seeing the bright blue sky on a clear day. I have been practicing my observation skills by stepping out of the fray and taking time to really look closely at one particular child or one area of the room. It makes me realize how much I miss when I'm only looking at the surface. —**Becky, preschool teacher**

I am struck by the last line about the time it takes to have a friend. It relates so much to what we have been studying in this class. To be with children and ourselves in meaningful ways takes time. I want to slow down and have enough time to form relationships with what I see, with the children and grown-ups around me, and with myself. —**LaVonda, ECE student**

Art of Awareness Activity

Draw the Contours: In *Learning by Heart*, Corita Kent recommends the use of contour drawings to enhance our ability to see things as artists do. When we look at the world and label its phenomena we often make immediate appraisals. We like something or dislike it. We accept it or reject it according to our ideas about its usefulness to us. We judge it based on some criteria from our past experiences. But to really see takes time and letting go of all of our preconceived notions. One of the ways artists cultivate their ability to see is using contour drawings. Contour drawings are made with keen attention on the object to be drawn, not looking at your paper or the drawing you are making. This practice develops your ability to see and ultimately enhances your ability to draw.

Creating and analyzing are two different processes and can't be done at the same time. This is true about contour drawing and also about observing children. It is impossible to really observe and see what is there when you are attempting to analyze what is happening at the same time. To practice letting go of analysis when you observe, try to let go of your expectations of the outcome for your drawing. Concentrate on learning to see the many details of the object you are trying to draw. Do this drawing very slowly. Begin by trying to see your hand as you draw its contours.

1. Find a place where you can be uninterrupted for at least fifteen minutes.
2. Sit at a table that is a comfortable drawing height, with a piece of paper on the table in front of you. You may want to tape the paper down so it doesn't move while you draw.
3. Put the point of your pen or pencil on the paper in front of you, and turn your body away from the paper so that you can see the hand you are not using to draw with, without being able to look at what you are drawing.
4. Pick some part of your hand to start with, and let your eye follow the outline and details of your hand. Your eye must move very slowly. At the same time, move the pencil point along the paper, reproducing every tiny detail of the line of your hand as your eye follows it. Be careful not to let either your eye or the pencil get ahead.
5. Rather than seeing "your hand," look at the the forms and lines your hand is made up of. Draw the details of what you see without looking at the paper or lifting your pencil point until you are done.
6. Reflect on your experience. How did it feel to draw without looking? Were you able to look closely at the details of your hand and let your pencil follow slowly?

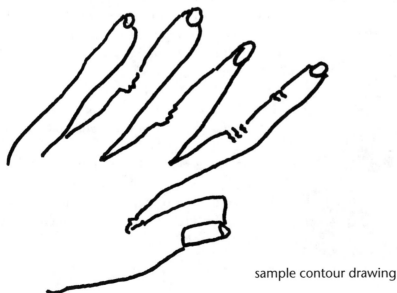

sample contour drawing

Learn to See Childhood As a Time of Building Relationships

The significant people and the time we spent with them are probably our most meaningful childhood experiences. Everything we know about children says that the best way for them to grow up is within a loving, nurturing family and community. In the world of "professional" early childhood programs we describe these experiences in the following ways:

- Developing social skills
- Building self-esteem
- Learning strategies to ease separation anxiety
- Getting techniques for guidance and discipline
- Managing conflict

Instead of adopting the clinical mindset revealed in these terms, we should focus our attention on the friendships and conflicts that are unfolding with the children. A prepackaged curriculum can't develop self-esteem. A checklist of social skills won't help children make friends, and a set of steps to follow is not a magic fix-it for conflicts and chaos. As professionals, we have to be vigilant that we don't reduce these important experiences and connections to the jargon of professional discourse, assessment checklists, and management techniques.

A better strategy is to call on the memories of our own meaningful relationships and seek to create similar conditions that foster connections and feelings in our daily work with children. The next activity will help you remember a heartfelt relationship you had as a child.

Practice Remembering an Important Relationship

Choose a particular person from your childhood who had a positive and significant influence on your life. This can be a grown-up or another child. Think about that person and describe the person in as much detail as you can remember, using these questions to guide your memory. You can either write this on your own or talk with a partner or small group.

- Describe this person's physical appearance: hands, hair, eyes, smell, clothing, tone of voice, and body language.
- What did you do together?
- What did this person do well and how did this person share himself with you?
- How did this person express affection or love for you?
- How did you feel about yourself when you were with this person? Why?

- What did you learn both directly and indirectly from this person that stays with you to this day?
- Think about your own relationships with children in your group. In what ways are you sharing yourself with them like this person did with you?

Practice Remembering a Childhood Conflict

Our challenge in observing children's conflicts is to identify our own tension and discomfort that often comes from past experiences or preconceptions about conflict situations. To see these moments clearly, we need to become aware of the personal baggage that could be clouding our view. The next activity will help you reflect on these issues.

Think back to your childhood and remember some incidents where you were involved with a conflict or observed a conflict in your family. If you have abuse or extreme experiences of pain or hurt in your childhood, you can choose to skip this activity. Such experiences should be healed through counseling or other personal work, however, so that they don't interfere with your ability to see children's conflicts clearly for what they are.

- What happened in the conflict you remember? What did people do or say?
- How did people respond to your expression of feelings?
- What did you learn about conflict from your experiences and what people said to you, either directly or indirectly?
- How do you think about conflict now?
- How do you think your childhood experiences and messages influence your responses to conflict now?

Observation Practice

Use the insights from your own memory of a special relationship to examine the following examples of observations of children involved in developing relationships with each other and with adults.

Movin' to Marco

Ten-month-old Tanisa is playing on the carpeted area in the infant room with a bucket of plastic toys. She pulls a rattle out of the bucket, looks at it, and puts it in her mouth. As she moves it away from her mouth, the rattle makes a noise. Her eyes brighten and she begins to shake it to hear more noise. As she watches herself wave the rattle about, she notices five-month-old Marco lying on the ground under a hanging mobile toy happily waving his arms and legs.

Tanisa crawls over to Marco and thrusts the rattle toward him. The hanging mobile is in her way and she can't get the rattle close enough to him. She barrels her way under the legs of the mobile, tipping it over, trying to get closer. A care-giver quickly comes over, picks up Marco, carries him to a baby seat across the carpet, and straps him in. She then puts a bucket of toys in front of where Tanisa is left sitting.

Tanisa looks down at the toys in the bucket and absently picks up a plastic cup. She shakes it, turns it over, and then puts the round end of it in her mouth. She looks toward Marco and her face lights up. She drops the cup and rapidly scoots across the carpet heading for him. When she reaches him, she heartily pulls herself up onto his baby seat reaching for his face with her open palm. Just before she can grab his nose, she tumbles on top of him.

Marco's eyes grow big and bright as he sees Tanisa's smiling face 2 inches from his own. The caregiver intervenes again, disentangling Tanisa, and pick-ing up Marco and holding him while she puts the bucket of toys back in front of Tanisa. Tanisa begins exploring the items in the bucket again as the caregiver takes Marco to the changing area.

We Can Get Along

Doug, five years old, is working in the block area on an elaborate construc-tion with the unit blocks. His building is about 3 feet square and 2 feet tall. He

arranges the blocks alternately by length and then by width. As he is carefully stacking a tower of blocks in the center of the structure, Saul, four years old, sits down next to him.

Saul watches Doug work for a while and then tentatively moves closer to the structure. With a worried look on his face, Saul deliberately knocks a corner of the building over. Doug begins to whine loudly, "Hey, don't do that! Teacher, he wrecked my building."

The teacher, who is watching nearby, comes closer and talks with the boys, "I don't blame you for being upset, Doug. You were working on an amazing structure and now it's ruined. Saul, it looked to me like what you really want to do is play with Doug. Is that why you knocked his building over?" Saul nods yes, still looking wor-ried. She continues, "Doug, Saul just wanted to play and I don't think he knew how to ask you. Maybe you could tell him your ideas about your building and he could help."

Doug smiles warmly at Saul and says, "Hey buddy, you can play." He begins demonstrating how he wants the blocks placed on the structure as he explains, "Here, build on this part." Saul adds some blocks as Doug has demonstrated. "Hey look buddy, is this the way?" Saul asks. "Yup, that looks good!" Doug responds. They look at each other with satisfied grins on their faces. Spontane-ously they wrap their arms around each other in a big hug.

Work alone or with a partner or small group to reflect on the two stories. Use these questions to guide your discussion:

– What is the children's point of view in each of these stories?
– How do they see their connections and relationships with others?
– What do each of these children already know and understand about forming connections and developing relationships?

In the first observation, the caregiver's concern for safety dominates this infant room. Obviously, safety is an important consideration of infant/toddler care. These babies need her attention to be safe and healthy. But what is she missing when she neglects the opportunities for social relationships and connections? Did you notice Tanisa's exuberant attempts to get to Marco? Tanisa wanted to play with him by showing him her rattle. She wanted to be near him, to look at him, and touch him. Did you notice the eager attention Marco had for Tanisa, even at his young age? How could the caregiver find a way for these babies to stay safe while nurturing their eagerness to connect? How can we negotiate safety issues with other important moments of childhood?

Adults often respond to children's conflict from our own sense of justice and fairness, which is often quite different from what children want in a given situation. We often underestimate children's ability to work things out, even when they are infants. We forget to look for the underlying motivations of the behaviors in question.

In the second observation, Saul and Doug's teacher has been conscientiously observing these children. She sees her role not as "fixing" their feelings or problems but as making visible what she sees. Her "help" comes in the form of offering trust and respect to let the children know they can work things out themselves. She pays close attention to Saul's body language and facial expressions and tries to put herself in his shoes. Her best guess about what is going on for him is that he wants to play and he doesn't know how to go about it. She offers Doug the chance to be compassionate and helpful, believing that children have great capacity for these feelings.

In this situation the teacher has invited the boys to see the possibilities for friendship rather than reminding them of rules. With their spontaneous hug the boys demonstrate the larger meaning of this moment—their ability to connect with each other and become friends. Their faces show us the joy that this brings.

I Want My Dolly Back!

Jill, the teacher in the toddler room, is sitting on the carpet with Angelic and Krystal as they play with a soft, stuffed elephant together. Karl wanders over and sits facing Angelic. He sees the stuffed elephant and reaches for it. Angelic lets out a piercing scream, "No," as she clutches the elephant tighter.

Teacher Jill urges Karl to ask Angelic if he can play too. He looks at her and asks, "Me play!" Angelic screeches angrily in Karl's face, "No." Karl punches her in the arm and grabs the elephant. Both children hold on for dear life and a tug-of-war ensues.

Angelic begins kicking Karl and hitting him with her free hand, screaming, "I want my dolly back. I want my dolly back." He responds by hitting her back several times.

Krystal, an onlooker to this point, punches Karl from the other side. He begins to flail his free arm in her direction, still holding on to the elephant. Krystal responds by kicking him over and over again.

Having watched this unfold in a matter of seconds, Teacher Jill lifts Krystal to her side, away from the fray, and then disengages Karl's hand from the elephant. Karl crawls away from the scene. As he turns to go, Teacher Jill begins to speak to him. He looks straight into her face and makes a fierce growling shout, drowning out what she is trying to tell him.

Jill turns her attention back to Krystal and Angelic who are both involved in nonstop crying. They are crying in unison, following each other's long, woeful moans. Teacher Jill suggests, "Would you like to go to the mirror and look at your sad faces? You are both so sad." They get up and go to the mirror, still lamenting, but now watching their own facial expressions as they cry. "Look at how sad your faces are. You even have tears," Jill points out. Karl joins them at the mirror, looking quizzically at the girls' faces along with them.

Work alone, with a partner, or in a small group to discuss the details of this story to find the meaning. Put yourself in each of these children's shoes, using the following questions as a guide.

– What do each of the children seem to understand about the situation?
– What do each of them feel strongly about?
– What strategies do they use to get what they want?
– What did you learn about each of the children from the details?
– What is your reaction to how the teacher handled this situation?
– How do you think the children felt about the teacher's response?

In the midst of a conflict, especially when children are screaming, crying, hitting, and kicking, many teachers find their hearts start to pound. Our heads fill with adult sentiments of justice and fairness, our serious responsibility to keep children safe, and our duty to teach them how they should behave and get along. Buried beneath all these thoughts are the responses we learned from our own childhoods, messages we received about expressing strong feelings and taking part in conflicts. Needless to say, it is extremely difficult to get past our own filters and bias to the current children's perspectives and understandings.

Throughout this book you have heard the message that childhood is a time of wonder. It is also a time of raw, uncensored emotions, a time of uncertainty, insecurity, and many fears. The ability to observe conscientiously, looking for children's points of view and understandings is critical in these situations. During intense incidents such as the one described above, children are constructing ideas about who they are. In essence, they are forming their identities. Teachers need to approach conflicts as clearly and openly as we can to help children through these scary times.

Take some time to study how teacher Jill is approaching this tumultuous incident.

Jill sees her role in this conflict as a storyteller, attempting to make the children's ideas and feelings visible. She doesn't try to fix their behavior or emotions. She tries to keep the children physically safe as best she can. And rather than pursuing who was right or wrong, she follows the most prominent theme, the crying girls. Thoughtfully, she tells and shows them the story of their own feelings, and in the process, helps them see each other's more clearly. This gets Karl's attention without her having to single him out as a perpetrator of hurtful behavior. For toddlers this is the most meaningful place to begin conflict negotiation, with their feelings.

Teachers can negotiate these difficult times, along with the joyful moments, by continually being mindful of their own mental filters and bias and focusing on the children's perspectives and understandings. Children have the right to wrestle through the difficult moments of childhood with adult respect and support for the full expression of their strong feelings.

Take Another Look

Most teachers are very invested in helping children learn to get along, feel accepted, and solve conflicts. Because this is an area of human development where emotions run deep for both adults and children, it is one that benefits from ongoing study and reflection. Here are some suggestions.

Observe Children Finding Playmates

Pick a child who enters play with others easily and one who struggles with this to observe over the course of a week or so. Watch as they approach or are approached in play situations, indoors and out. How do they respond? What words, body language, and strategies do they use? Write down the details and compare the differences between the two children.

Observe the Language of Friendship

Choose a small group of children who typically play together. Listen and record their conversations and interactions related to their friendships. Remember to notice the language of gesture and negotiations. Do you hear any repeated phrases that indicate their efforts to understand what it means to be a friend?

Remember to seek their point of view, rather than your agenda for how they should be behaving.

Observe for Conflicts and Problem Solving

Make note of the conflicts that occur among the children in your group over the course of a week. Try to analyze each by looking for the details and the children's point of view, using the following questions to guide your thinking.

– Are there any patterns in the sources of these conflicts?
– What seem to be the children's understandings?
– What strategies do they use to get what they want?
– Notice and reflect on your own reactions to these conflicts and interactions. Is there anything from your own childhood that influences how you see these situations?

More Things to Do

As you work to see children's relationships more closely, also devote time to explore your own experience with developing relationships. This will give you more insight into this process with children.

Think of a Friendship You've Developed As an Adult

Identify someone outside of your family with whom you've developed a friendship as an adult. Try to remember how this happened. What kinds of things did you do together that helped you become friends? How did you spend time together? What did you offer each other? How have you handled differences between you? What helped develop trust and affection?

Remember Difficult Moments in Relationships

All of us have had times with other people when things didn't go well. As you recall particular experiences, consider how you felt and what you tried to do to resolve the situation. See if you can uncover any new insights into children's behaviors. Try using this list to organize your memories.

– Remember a time when your feelings were hurt by someone you trusted.
– Remember a time that you broke something that belonged to someone else.

– Remember a time when you were rebuffed or excluded from a relationship or activity.
– Remember a time when you were tricked or lied to.
– Remember a time when you felt misunderstood.

Practice More Contour Drawings

To continue expanding your ability to see details, do at least ten more contour drawings as described early in the Art of Awareness section of this chapter.

Recommended Resources

Levin, Diane, and Nancy Carlsson-Paige. *Best Day of the Week* and *Before Push Comes to Shove. Building Conflict Resolution Skills with Children.* St. Paul: Redleaf Press, 1998. *Best Day of the Week* is a children's book about children's points of view in conflict situations. *Before Push Comes to Shove* is a teacher's guide that helps adults analyze the story and use strategies to guide children in using their own perspectives about conflict.

Paley, Vivian. *You Can't Say You Can't Play.* Cambridge, Massachusetts: Harvard University Press, 1992. In this fascinating look at the moral dimensions of the classroom, Paley introduces a new rule, "You can't say you can't play," to her kindergarten students. The story unfolds as Paley, in her usual fashion, enables readers to share a child's view of the world.

———. *The Kindness of Children.* Cambridge: Harvard University Press, 1998. Here is a remarkable collection of stories that show children's abilities to offer kindness, sensitivity, and support to others.

10

STUDY SESSION

Observing Children
with Their Families

There is nothing more touching to me than a family picture where every-one is trying to look his or her best, but you can see what a mess they all really are. Frozen in the amber of the photograph, you can see all the connections and disconnections, the stress and the yearning. And you can see the pride in their lineage—in that big bottom lip, say, that went from grandma to dad to baby. It's there on their faces for all to see and you see how they love it—that big lip. It is their immortality.

Anne Lamott

Learning Goals for This Study Session

In this study session you will

- Practice using mirrors to take different perspectives.
- Recall the influences of your family and family life on your attitudes and values.
- Examine the similarities and differences of values and attitudes between you and the families you work with.
- Practice observing the details of children's connections with their family.
- Practice seeing a parent's point of view.

Reflect on the Quote

Reflect on the quotation from Anne Lamott. What does it mean to you? How does it relate to your work with children? Do some reflective writing or discuss this with others. Consider this example of a teacher's reflections on what it meant to her.

> The first time I read this through, I thought she was being disrespectful to family life. When I read it again, I realized how much I want to romanticize family life and that what she is saying is really true. Yes, we have pride and loyalties in our families and that's good, but we all have things that are nuts too, and often we don't like to admit that. I hope I can remember this when some of the families of my kids seem like such a loose show. Maybe I can have more empathy if I think of them as a family picture on the shelf of life.
> —Cheryl, teacher

Art of Awareness Activity

Explore Mirrors: Working with mirrors offers the opportunity to explore visual perceptions in interesting ways. For young children, this actually develops their brains so that they more easily see things from different points of view. When adults use mirrors, as in the following exercise, we too stretch our brains' capacity to see different perspectives.

1. Gather a collection of mirrors of different sizes and shapes. Mylar mirror papers are good to include as well. Try the following activities using your mirrors.

2. Hold two of the mirrors together at a right angle with the edges touching so that you can open and close them like a book. Hold the mirrors close enough to see an image of your face across both mirrors. Slowly open and close the mirrors, watching for a progressive number of images of yourself.

3. Place a mirror perpendicular to a piece of paper on a table in front of you. Try writing your name on the paper looking only in the mirror as you write.

4. On another piece of paper draw a wavelike line, and then looking only in the mirror, try to trace the line on the paper with your finger.

5. Now try using pattern blocks to create a design while looking in the mirror. Pay attention to the duplicate image you see in your mirror and use that to guide the development of your design.

Take some time to write about or discuss your experience with a partner or small group. What did you notice was easy or difficult for you? How do you think this relates to the process of becoming aware of seeing things from different perspectives?

Learn to See Childhood As a Time for Strong Family Connections

Each of the mirror experiences above asks you to try seeing things in ways that aren't typical. This is exactly what you need to learn when observing and working with children and their families.

Childhood is a time of experiencing yourself as part of a family. In their families children get nicknames, hear who they look like, what their grandma used to do, and what they themselves did when they were younger. A sense of history and identity evolves through these interactions and stories. Unless we understand these family settings we can't really know the full measure of a child nor provide continuity for them when they are with us.

Each child is born into a family that has its own values, customs, and internal dynamics. Whatever the family makeup or circumstances, all parents start off with hopes and dreams for their child. There is not always a conscious awareness of this, nor of the family traditions and patterns that will be strongly influencing the child, but they are there nonetheless. Often it is an unexamined way of being that shapes a child and creates a sense of identity and belonging.

When a family enrolls their child in one of our programs we are often concerned with how they will separate from the family and bond with the new caregivers. Separation anxiety is the focus of a great number of staff discussions and workshops. As we begin to recognize that children today are spending more of their waking hours in our programs than with their families, we should be working to help children stay connected to their families, rather than focus on their separation.

Whatever level of diversity in your program, it is important not to assume that staff and parents share common perspectives and values with regard to child rearing practices. Differences may exist as a result of personal preference, culture, economic conditions, life experiences, and age or generation factors and thus may result in misunderstandings, if not judgments of each other. To build strong partnerships with children's families, you can apply the same awareness and observation skills you use with children to discover indicators of family values, traditions, and communication styles. Approaching families with a mindset of curiosity, suspended judgment, and eagerness to learn will help you build trust and will support the needed continuity and connections between children and their families.

Just as your view of children's behaviors can be clouded by your own childhood experiences, your view of their relationships with their families can be similarly obscured. Remembering adult influences that supported your identity development will help you value the ways that families support their children's identities. Use the following activity to reflect on your own childhood influences.

Practice Identifying Affirming Connections in Your Childhood

Think about the people in your family or close circle of friends that had strong, affirming influences on you as you were growing up. Whether you grew up with

your biological family or in a foster or surrogate family, or even if you didn't have a warm or close family experience, consider one particular person from your childhood who had a very positive influence on you. Use these questions to help you describe this person either in writing or to a partner or small group.

– Describe the person's hands, voice, smell, and clothing.
– What did this person share with you?
– What did this person do well?
– How did this person let you know you were loved and cared for?
– What can you say that this person taught you about life that still influences you today?

Next consider the traditions of your family or close friends. What are some of the most touching and important rituals, values, and activities that came from your past experiences with these people that you have developed and kept alive through the years?

Reflect on these two memory activities and think about the values and beliefs you bring to your work with young children. Are these the same as or different from what you know about the families of the children you work with? What are the shared values and experiences that you have with the families? What differences do you see in your values and experiences? How can you account for these differences?

Observation Practice

Using your new awareness about your own family experiences, see what else you can discover from these observation stories about children's relationships with their families.

A Game about Good-bye

A small group of children created a forest on one of the building platforms in the block area. They stood small logs on ends for trees, used blue scarves to create a lake and a waterfall, lined up small rocks to make paths, and built a castle with colorful foam blocks. They added animal families, many parents and children all around the castle, and the forest. After a few minutes of sorting out the characters, a game evolved. The animal parents gathered their babies together in the forest and said, "We're going on a long trip. You stay here." The animal children began to cry when their parents left. The parents called out to them, "We're going to work, but we'll be home soon." While the parents were at work they called the children on the phone to say, "We're coming home now!" The children and parents rejoiced when they returned to the castle.

After repeating this drama over and over again, one of the children intensified the game. "You hafta tell my baby giraffe that her mommy is died and is going to stay died for one week." The giraffe baby cried and cried and the other animals cried. The other adult animals offered, "I'll take care of you, baby giraffe." "You can live with my family, giraffe baby." In the midst of this comfort the mama giraffe returned: "Good news! The mama came alive again!"

Work on your own, with a partner, or in a small group to discuss this story. What are the children showing they are concerned about in this play? How are they using the toys and materials to represent their issues? What do their conversations tell you about their mutual concerns and understandings of family life? What are the underlying themes and meaning of this drama for the children?

This story helps us see the important role we have in helping children stay connected to their families. Children rely on grown-ups, particularly their family members, for all of their sense of belonging, security, and comfort needs. This is why separation from their families is such a big issue in their lives. When you observe them closely you can see the many ways they explore their fears and create opportunities to gain comfort and security.

Did you notice the way the children in this story used the materials to create a comfy, safe, and beautiful environment for the animal families? Children will often create these kinds of representations in their play activities, seemingly to reassure and comfort themselves. Does the children's play around death cause you to be uncomfortable? Can you see how this part of the drama adds to their own power and competence over their fears?

Children act out their worst fears and fantasies so they have the opportunity to resolve them and come to their own rescue. In the drama above the children used their game to explore the grieving themes of good-bye in daily life and in death. When you are aware and accept children's issues and understandings it will help you find more ways to reassure them while they are away from their families.

Take Me Out to the Ball Game

Ever since the first day in his child care program, Casey has worn a hat or T-shirt with the logo of his favorite baseball team. His mom and dad often do the same. Yesterday they picked him up together, greeting him with "Hey, Slugger," and tossing him a mitt. They talked excitedly about his mom and dad's softball team and who would be pitching that night.

Today at the playdough table Casey has made a baseball field, rolling long pieces to create a diamond and flat ones for the bases. He gets three corks out of the basket and says they are his mom, dad, and himself, all baseball players on the same team. He begins to act out a drama on the field with his cork players. He announces excitedly, "The mom throws the pitch. The dad hits a high fly ball, deep to center field. Casey goes back … back … back … he leaps up, the crowd cheers, and yes, he makes an amazing catch!"

Work on your own or with a partner or small group using the following questions to think more about Casey and his family:

– In what ways do you see this family's passion for baseball influencing Casey?
– What is Casey's view of his family and his perspective of himself in his family?
– What do you think he is learning from his family?

Whether you're a baseball fan or not, it's important to respect the influence that these family experiences have on Casey. Observing children with their families and noticing family influences on children's play gives teachers useful insight into the child's perspective. Can you see how this shared experience with his family brings great joy and a strong sense of positive identity to Casey? The brief glimpse we get of his activities around baseball show the opportunities for language and creative representation that these meaningful family experiences offer him. He brings these as a foundation for learning as he plays in his child care program. Family life is a rich source of curriculum that teachers can observe and use for planning relevant activities.

Here are two additional stories that can be read and thought about together because they suggest a similar pattern of cross-cultural tension over different values and perspectives.

Stay Out of the Sand

Melissa, a child care teacher, believes kids learn by exploring freely, even if they do get a bit dirty in the process. She encourages the kids to play to their hearts' content when they are outside using the wonderful playground the center worked so hard to build. One of the parents has been complaining, however: "I don't want my daughter playing in your sandbox. I spent an hour and a half fixing her hair and two minutes after she's outside, her hair is filled with sand. I can't get that stuff out and we spend our whole evening trying to clean it up. So, please, keep her away from that sandbox and any other place on the playground where she's going to get dirty."

Potty Time

A mother and a caregiver are engaged in an intense discussion. "I just can't do what you want," says the caregiver. "I don't have time with all of these other children to care for. Besides, I don't believe in toilet training a one year old."

"But she's already potty trained!" the mother says emphatically. "All you have to do is put her on the potty."

"I really don't think she's trained." The caregiver's voice is still calm, but a red flush is beginning to creep up her neck and toward her face.

"You just don't understand," says the mother, picking up her daughter and diaper bag and sweeping out the door.

"No, you're the one who doesn't understand," mutters the caregiver, busying herself with a pile of toys on the floor.

At the beginning of these study sessions you reflected on the meaning of these words from Lisa Delpit, which are worth reviewing again:

> *"We do not really see through our eyes or hear through our ears, but through our beliefs. To put our beliefs on hold is to cease to exist as ourselves for a moment."*

Whether you support or disagree with the parent's or the caregiver's perspectives in these stories, try applying the ideas from Delpit when exploring the meaning of what is unfolding in these stories. Work on your own, with a partner, or with a small group using the following questions:

- What specific details in this story give you information about each person's perspective?
- What do the details indicate that each person values and cares about?
- How might you summarize the contrast in their differing perspectives?

In each of the earlier study sessions of this book you have been asked to develop an awareness of your own mental filters and point of view and to try to take the perspectives of the children you are observing. Grounded in that development, you can use the same principles to try to see the point of view of other adults. Trying to put yourself in the parents' shoes and see situations from their interests and needs will build trust and respect between you.

There are a number of resources to help you better understand how to work cross-culturally. A good starting place is with the work of college teacher and author Janet Gonzalez-Mena, who writes about cultural assumptions and misunderstandings that pervade early childhood programs. Most of our professional standards and knowledge base about good early childhood practice has been developed from a European American perspective. Rules we make about what children need and how they should be cared for and interacted with stem from a particular perspective and set of values. As our programs include increasing diversity along the lines of culture, class, language, family structure, and disability, among others, we need to take care not to assume that there is one right way of doing things and that the parents should conform to the teacher's point of view. As you work to sensitize yourself to cross-cultural issues, keep the following questions in mind for assessing your observations:

– What are my assumptions about the best way to handle this situation?
– What values are influencing my point of view?
– What evidence do I see that another set of values or assumptions are at work with this child and family?
– How can I find out more about their point of view in a respectful, sensitive way?

Take Another Look

There are a number of ways you can heighten your awareness of children in the context of their families. These activities will help you explore possible strategies to use throughout your teaching days.

Be Alert to How Children Think about Their Families

Every day in your program children incorporate feelings and themes from their family life into their play and representations. Over a week's time gather a collection of observations and representations that reveal how children are thinking about family life. They may do this through dress up and direct role-plays, pretending to be human or animal family members, or they may create family scenes with props as they build or play around the room. Watch and listen for what they are creating in the art area, when they have conversations, make up rhymes and songs. Looking over your week's collection, see if you can recognize any patterns or themes in your observation notes. Discuss these with coworkers to expand your understanding with other points of view.

Watch for Family Interests, Customs, and Rituals

Observe a child and family member together every day for a week or so, at either drop-off or pickup time. Notice their body language and communication style. Do they have any routines or rituals that they do day after day? Do they talk about their interests or activities? How do they greet and say good-bye to each other? How do they express emotions with each other? Do they communicate primarily through body language or with words? What details can you describe that informs you about their point of view about these interactions?

If at all possible, try visiting the family at home for an even closer look at family, interests, customs, and patterns. When this is approached as a way to strengthen partnerships, rather than a requirement to gather information, families are often receptive and appreciative.

Create Family Books

Most of the paperwork we have families complete when they enroll their child is impersonal and of limited use in helping us understand their family life. A more meaningful complement to enrollment papers are pages for the child and family to complete and add to a classroom family book. Try creating a simple form for sharing some initial information, such as pictures and stories of something special about each person in the family, something they like about where they live, someone the family admires and talks about. Suggest that the form be filled out together as a family, using words, drawings, or photos. Offer to send home a camera as needed. The following two pages have samples of forms that can be used for this purpose.

As the pages are brought to you, keep the family book in a prominent place where everyone can read it. Observe not only the information on the pages, but the way children talk about the information with each other. Notice if anything changes in the children's or families' conversations with each other. Does the family book give them a way to connect with each other? Does it serve as a springboard for more storytelling about family experiences?

As the year goes along you can send home more pages to be filled out, asking for stories about such things as the day the child was born, birthday or holiday celebrations, or hopes and dreams the family has.

Invite Family Members to Share Stories of Their Childhoods

Inviting family members to come and tell the children a story about their own childhoods is a great way to learn more about who they are, and it furthers the bonds between the children and their own families. Stories about their families also create new interest and friendships between the children themselves.

Offer a general invitation, in writing, in person, and over the phone, to visit the classroom with a childhood story. Be sure to welcome extended family members and ask if they are willing to have their story written down and illustrated by you and the children so that it can be preserved in a classroom book for ongoing enjoyment.

As family members visit, you get another opportunity to observe, hear, and support their connections with their child. Notice how your own relationship with them continues to deepen as well. When time permits reflect on what you are learning, either in writing, or with a coworker.

Child's Name_____ Birthday_____

How I got my name

Something I love to do

What I look like

Something
I want to learn

What makes me happy   What makes me sad or mad

Family Name_____

Who's in our family

Something special about each
person in our family

Someone our family admires
and talks about

Something we
like about where we live

A favorite story we tell in our family

More Things to Do

As you develop strategies to involve and observe children with their families, remember to continue developing your own ability to see other perspectives.

Standing in Another's Shoes

To practice taking another person's perspective, try out the following scenarios on your own or with a small group, and then reflect on what happened using the questions that follow.

Situation: After a beautiful sunny morning it begins raining really hard around noon. Act out the scene using the phrase "It's raining," from each of these perspectives.

- A farmer who has just finished planting seeds
- A school child who has been working in class all morning and has been looking forward to recess
- A weather reporter

Situation: A child discovers a large mud puddle on the playground and is splashing joyfully in it. Act out the scene and use the phrase "What are you doing?" from each of these perspectives.

- The teacher who is supervising the playground
- A parent who has come to pick the child up
- Another child

The points of view and differences in the responses above are obvious, but how aware of this are you in your everyday work life? Continue exploring this idea by writing or sharing a story with a partner or small group about a time you had a completely different point of view from another person as you shared the same experience. Describe what happened and all of the possible perspectives of those involved.

Share Memories of "How We Did It"

To explore your own values and how they might be different from the families you work with, try this activity. In writing or with a partner or small group, describe how something was done in your family in areas such as health care, meal preparation, and discipline. As you compare your experiences with others in your group, see if this gives you insight into different approaches families in your program may be taking in this area.

Recommended Resources

Alvarado, Cecelia, et al. *In Our Own Way. How Anti-Bias Work Shapes Our Lives.* St Paul: Redleaf Press, 1999. A collection of personal essays describing the different life experiences that have led the authors to a deeper understanding of how bias shapes cross-cultural perspectives.

California Tomorrow. *Looking in, Looking Out. Redefining Child Care and Early Education in a Diverse Society.* San Francisco: California Tomorrow, 1996. A comprehensive report of research interviews exploring how early childhood programs can meet the needs of diverse families.

Cortez, Jesus, et al. *Infant and Toddler Caregiving. A Guide to Culturally Sensitive Care.* San Francisco: Center for Child and Family Studies; Far West Laboratory for Educational Research and Development, 1991. This is a companion guide to the video *Essential Connections: Ten Keys to Culturally Sensitive Child Care,* which describes the importance of culture in early development and offers a variety of practical examples to help programs become culturally sensitive with their families.

Delpit, Lisa. *Other People's Children. Cultural Conflict in the Classroom.* New York: The New Press, 1995. A book of essays that urge us to stand in the other person's shoes. A probing look at the cultural conflicts in schools that come from our own filters and bias.

Fialka, Janice. *It Matters. Lessons from My Son.* Self-published, 1998. A collection of poems and prose honestly describing the range of feelings and experiences of being a parent of a child with special needs.

Gonzalez-Mena, Janet. *Multi-Cultural Issues in Child Care.* Mountain View, California: Mayfield Press, 1993. The stories in this book provide great examples of children in the context of families with different cultural values.

Hannigan. *Off to School. A Parent's-Eye View of the Kindergarten Year.* Washington, D.C.: NAEYC. A parent shares some of her own journal entries along with messages from her son's teacher. A warm and informative set of communications that build partnerships and increase understandings.

Rodriguez, Richard. *Hunger of Memory.* New York: Bantam, 1983. This book offers a clear taste of the confusion and loss that occurs for children of color who become assimilated into the dominant culture without retaining a strong positive identity and connection to their family, culture, and language.

Williams, Leslie, and Yvonne DeGaetano. *Alerta: A Multicultural Bilingual Approach to Teaching Young Children.* Menlo Park, California: Addison Wesley, 1985. An extremely useful book about creating programs for bilingual, bicultural families. There are concrete ideas, forms, and handouts that can guide you in learning the perspectives of the families in your programs.

Using Your Observations

11

Observation can be used not only as the basis of information about individual children and the building of a classroom community, but also as the place from which teachers can begin to engage in the dialogic process of reflection, hypothesis building, and planning.

Gretchen Reynolds and Elizabeth Jones

Because there are so many pressures and demands on teachers, it's easy to think of gathering observations as just another accountability system. But if you take the approach suggested in this book, you will quickly discover that the process begins to enhance your teaching in numerous ways. The act of becoming more mindful in your teaching keeps you in tune with how you are feeling and what you are thinking, as well as what's going on with the children. Your job becomes more enjoyable, and you become more intentional in your planning and responses to children. Curriculum ideas begin to flow from what's actually meaningful to the children. The children's learning becomes more integrated and so does yours.

When you offer your observations back to the children themselves, you promote a self-reflection process in them. You give them more language and the early experience of "metacognition"—thinking about their thinking process. This enables them to consider what else they might do and to gain experience in naming their intentions. The children's ability to describe more details about their undertakings will enhance their connections between the classroom and their home life. Your own stories about their conversations and activities will further invite families to join you in thinking about their children. Rather than viewing them as another requirement, think of using your observations to enhance your own growth, the children's, and the partnership you want to develop with their families. Observing children will make your job better, easier, and more fun.

Observations Can Enhance Your Disposition, Knowledge, and Planning

Heightening your awareness through close observation helps you remember what you value about being with children. You can re-enter this precious time of life with a new approach, recognizing how brief it is, and how much you gain from noticing the details of what is unfolding. Paying attention in this way is emotionally nourishing. It also enhances your intellectual curiosity, sparks your interest in finding out more about a particular child and her development and learning process.

What you see and hear in your daily observations will give you a wealth of ideas for planning curriculum that is meaningful and relevant to the children's lives. You will find any number of seeds for growing valuable learning outcomes. Sometimes these will become extended in-depth curriculum projects, but often they are just ordinary moments that are reflections of the ongoing learning process children engage in.

Learn to Value Ordinary Moments

Once you tune in to the details of what children are doing and saying, you will often be astonished. They will show you how they are growing and changing, expanding their interests and know-how in the smallest of gestures. As you come to value this you will begin to feel each moment is important and worthy of recording, even the ones that seem "ordinary" at first glance. Of course, time and competing demands won't permit you to capture each moment in writing, and you will need to make choices about what to preserve. Perhaps you spot one of those many firsts or discover a pattern that a child is beginning to repeat again and again. Let these moments linger with you and share them with others. They are the stuff of the moment, the lives of children in the here and now, not some anticipated future you might not witness.

Descriptions of ordinary moments can be presented to others as sound-bite stories, alerting readers to how extraordinary the ordinary lives of children are. Here are a few examples from preschool teacher Sarah Felstiner.

October 8, 1997

Teacher Lisa jotted down this quote from Ben, said while he was sweeping up some birdseed. "I used to bop people, but I've changed. I learned not to and now

I don't bop anymore." Lisa asked, "How did you learn that?" Ben replied, "By seeing other people not bop each other."

October 13, 1997

While working with the Unifix cubes, Ben decided to create a pattern of colors: brown, orange, yellow, green, brown, orange, yellow, green, and so on.

December 1997

Emily carefully sang the alphabet song while she worked on writing these letters.

As you begin to collect observations of ordinary moments, you will discover the themes of childhood. Some of these were the focus of the study sessions of earlier chapters in this book. Over time you will find yourself with a treasure chest of examples of this remarkable time of life. There are many things you can go on to "do" with your observations, but first of all, just cherish them. They are gifts children are giving to you.

See Yourself As a Researcher

Sometimes things about children's behavior feel like a disappointment rather than a gift. They can irritate rather than delight you. These are the moments when we are tempted to label, if not punish, children. A more productive approach is to try to transform an irritation into something you are curious about, asking yourself questions like these:

– Why is this happening?
– What do I need to see that I don't yet understand?
– What is the underlying source and meaning of this behavior?

Viewing irritating behaviors as unfolding stories you don't yet understand can change your emotional reaction and the way you proceed with the children. If you see yourself as a researcher trying to find the meaning of particular play or conversation themes, this sharpens your focus for observing. Your stories about what you are seeing and hearing can draw others into the process, creating a collaborative project for teacher self-development and more focused conversations with parents.

Consider the example of some boys in the block area whose play has become active and loud as they race cars down ramps they have built. This escalates as they line up blocks to crash into at the bottom of the ramp, creating a domino effect. When no one is getting hurt and the children seem very involved in the play, should it be stopped because it's loud and irritating to the teachers?

Rather than give in to this knee-jerk reaction, Deb and her co-teacher, Rhonda Iten, turned this into a research project. They watched and listened closely to this irritating play, taking some notes and drawing sketches. One day, after the children had gone home, they went to the block area and used their documentation to recreate the children's ramp structures and began imitating the loud car crashing play. To their surprise, they discovered how exciting it was to adjust the ramp so the cars would go faster and to place the blocks just so at the end to create a crashing domino effect. They not only got insight into the emotional thrill involved, but also discovered what good engineers the children were. It took careful planning and placement to position the ramp and the blocks to create the domino effect. Now understanding the value of this loud, active play, the next day they returned to the children with a plan to provide more space and opportunity for this kind of play. They now knew how to offer helpful suggestions to keep this play productive, rather than outlawing it out of irritation or fear that it would get out of hand.

Using Your Observations to Plan

Observation notes are one of the most valuable resources you have for individual and group curriculum planning. Rather than arbitrarily choosing a theme to center your planning around, first consider what you have been seeing and hearing. Use the questions below to try to discover from your observations what seems most engaging to the children and how that might be further supported in your planning.

– What is the essence of this experience from the child's point of view?
– What does this child know and know how to do?
– What is this child exploring, experimenting with, or trying to figure out?
– What does this child find frustrating?
– How does this child feel about herself?

When you want to plan for individual children, you can study your observation notes for play themes and social, emotional, and cognitive patterns. Finding the interests and strengths of a child as the springboard of your planning will move you away from the prevailing "deficit model" of individualizing. It will help the child's family know that you are seeing fully and not just looking for possible problems or areas needing improvement.

You will also find it extremely useful to share your observations and thoughts about them with coworkers and the children's families. This will help them see how you go about planning from your observations. They will be reassured that even though your curriculum doesn't look like the school model they might be expecting, you are carefully planning and monitoring outcomes. For example, preschool teacher Sarah Felstiner does this by publicly posting an analysis of some observation notes next to some photos, conversation transcripts, and examples of the children's activities. Note how she "thinks aloud" for the benefit of herself and other adults who might be wondering where her curriculum plans are. She demonstrates accountability in a form that is ultimately more meaningful than putting names of activities in little boxes on a lesson plan schedule.

November 4

Looking back at these snippets of children's experiences over the past few months, I begin to see possibilities for an extended project around these ideas of hiding and trickery, ships and the Titanic, *sparkly things and treasure. Until now I've been watching and waiting, focusing the curriculum around group identity and artistic development, hoping for a strand of shared passion to bubble up from the collective interests of the class.*

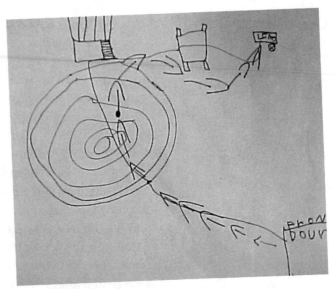

    Why is it valuable to choose a central focus like this? I find it intensifies children's work and interest, and brings them together with a communal sense of learning and exploration. Of course, we still enjoy building, drawing, drama, playdough, and all the other activities in the classroom, but we will also begin to focus more on activities and conversations about "Tricks, Treasures, and the Titanic.*" Children's play is incorporating these ideas naturally, but I will also be bringing in new materials and provoking experiences that highlight these themes. For example, I've already begun to provision treasurelike stones, beads, and coins, and collect resources about treasure, the* Titanic, *pirates, and more.*

    Why is it valuable to choose a theme that children are demonstrating an interest in? I find that children display a much higher level of energy and engagement for their work when it centers around subjects of their choosing. Though I will often bring in unrelated art activities, cooking projects, science experiments, and so on, I try to intersperse those with deep study around topics children are passionate about. In addition, I will try to extend that exploration for as long as possible, going deeper into certain areas, or letting the children's questions lead us off on new tangents.

A few weeks later Felstiner made another posting, telling the story of how her project ideas were progressing and the connections that were being made with a project on homelessness in the room across the hall.

Emily, Julia, and Zabia played a rather involved treasure game that seemed to reflect some of the ideas from the Uri Shulevitz story The Treasure, *which we had read the day before. I took pictures and recorded some of their words while they played, interested in the ways they were revisiting and revising the story.*

    I was particularly touched by the connection I saw to the work around collecting coins to give to homeless people that the Starlight class has been telling us about. I sensed the influence of that learning in their responses to the story about treasure. Shulevitz's story begins, "There once was a man and his name was Isaac. He lived in such poverty that again and again he went to bed hungry."

I am beginning to see a connection between the kind of treasure gathering, counting, and collecting that these children are doing in the block area, and the gathering of real coins they have undertaken as part of their exploration of home-lessness issues.

Analyzing your documentation helps you find underlying themes and connections between what the children are saying and doing with each other. Publicly articulating your thinking process solicits input from your coworkers and the children's families. This is a powerful way to keep your curriculum planning creative, relevant, and on target.

You can also use your observations to do individual planning and informal assessment. If you are required to complete assessment checklists on each child, consider basing these on your observation narratives. With detailed notes and photographs you can document the same progress in a much more engaging form. Compare the two options below, one from an assessment book and the other from the observation notes of Sarah Felstiner. Can you guess which one is likely to end up posted on the refrigerator and which on the floor of the family car?

MATH CONCEPTS CHECKLIST

☑ Sorts objects according to function, size, and shape

☑ Identifies circle, square, triangle, rectangle

☑ Exhibits an understanding of one-to-one correspondence

☑ Duplicates sequential order of objects or pictures

☑ Understands simple measurement techniques

January 10

In the studio this morning, Emily and some friends were working on making masks. Emily offered to help Alex attach some string to hold the mask on. She cut a piece of string, but it was too short to reach around Alex's head. She said, "Maybe this can be for Maria's mask, this extra string, 'cause she has a little face."

Emily cut another piece, but it was too long. She said, "How 'bout we cut half of it off and try it again?"

Both of these comments show a sophisticated understanding of relationships between length, circumference, and so on, as well as displaying Emily's thoughtfulness about her friends.

Take Another Look

If you watch closely, you'll discover stories like Sarah Felstiner's can be uncovered in any good early childhood program. Take time to practice using your observations as a way to enhance your teaching disposition, knowledge, and planning. Here are some ideas to try in your program.

Observe Self-Directed Skills

Watch a child of any age attempting some self-directed skill, be it sitting up, cutting, tying shoes, communicating a fear, trying to get a turn on the tire swing, or supporting a friend in need. Make notes about the strategies that were used. How are these the same as or different from what you've seen on other occasions? What are you curious about? What is worth marveling about here? Tell this as a story to others, orally or in writing.

Explain an Artwork

Look over a child's drawing or other creation and ask that child to explain it to you. Tell that explanation as a story to someone else, communicating what you understand to be most significant. Try this with several more people, children and adults, drawing out more details from the response you get to each telling.

Turn Annoyances into Research Questions

Brainstorm a list of questions, behaviors, or pieces of children's work that perplex or irritate you. Experiment with turning some of these concerns into questions, starting with phrases like, "why do . . ." or "how do . . ." Choose one of these question that appeals to you, and make a plan for when and how you might gather some observation notes about this. If you can interest others in this topic, invent a little research form and distribute it as a reminder to be recording observations on your question. A form might look as simple as the one on page 124.

After an agreed-upon period of time, gather with your fellow researchers and discuss your findings. Consider seeking out other professional resources on the topic in your ECE literature or on-line through the Educational Resources Information Center (ERIC) or on-line discussion groups such as the following:

- ECENET-L (subscribe at listserv@postoffice.cso.uiuc.edu)
- ECEOL-L (subscribe at listserv@maine.edu)
- REGGIO-L (subscribe at listserv@postoffice.cso.uiuc.edu)
- TAWL-Teachers Applying Whole Language
  (subscribe at listserv@listserv.arizona.edu)

Research Question: How do children use sounds in their play and what might this mean?

Date ____/____/____ Time _____

Details of the setting or context_____

Detailed description of children using sounds _____

Was this the first time you noticed this particular use of sound? _____

How is this observation similar to or different from other occasions?_____

Do you see any pattern or theme? _____

Hunches about the meaning? _____

Look for In-Depth Curriculum Themes

When you see children involved in some play or conversation over the course of several days, study your notes and photographs for possible underlying themes that could launch an in-depth curriculum project. Offer additional props to keep it going, along with descriptions and photos for the children to hear and see what you have noticed about their interest. Use their responses as input for what to do next. Post this as a story, along with photos and any transcripts of conversations as with the Sarah Felstiner example above.

Observations Can Stimulate Children's Learning

Documentation of observations can be used not just by the teachers, but by the children themselves. Children benefit enormously from hearing your stories about them and seeing evidence of what they have been doing. This enhances their self-esteem and their connections with each other. When children are vividly reminded of what they have been doing, it often stimulates them to go further with an idea, expanding or deepening their pursuits, sometimes encountering the need for a cognitive or emotional leap. Preschool teacher Ann Pelo describes it this way:

> As children reflect on their earlier play, as they revisit their
> work, they can think in new ways about their experiences, just
> as we adults hone our thinking by study and reflection over

time. They may have conversations with each other in which they use their earlier experiences as launching pads into new learning. They may decide to repeat an earlier experience, to get it clear in their minds. They may tell the story of the experience to someone who was not involved.

"Hey, look at that photo! Remember when we made that rocket ship with blocks? Let's make it again!"

"What do those words say?"

"They say, 'Casey sorted the dinosaurs into two groups: a group of mommies and a group of daddies.'"

"Oh, yeah, I did that! I'm going to make more groups today: brothers and sisters."

"Why did you make that drawing?"

"Well, I wanted to show how I looked when I was dressed up like a princess. See, we were playing a game about a king and queen, and I wanted to join the game, but Tara said I had to be a princess. First, I didn't want to be. Then, Stu found a crown for me to wear and then I wanted to be the princess."

You can use your circle or meeting time to share stories about what you have seen them doing. Some of these can be put into little books, read to them, and put in the book area for them to be read independently by the children. Sketches or photographs with sound bite stories of your observations can be placed on bulletin boards, on room dividers, or in Plexiglas frames on shelves of the area where they took place. As this becomes a regular practice the children will refer to this documentation to remind each other of what they have done, or to remember how to approach a particular activity again. As a result, they continue to practice skills, expanding their vocabulary and their sense of belonging.

Take Another Look

It's worth experimenting with different ways to use your observation stories with the children themselves. Choose a couple of the following ideas to try in your program. Do them repeatedly over the course of a month and make note of how the children begin to refer to them or initiate similar observation or storytelling activities themselves.

Sketch Children's Work

Have a collection of clipboards, pens, and paper readily accessible in the room. When you see children doing some building with Lego plastic building blocks, wood blocks, or scrap materials, use a clipboard to sit and sketch what they are making. Talk about this with the children and post it near the area where it happened.

Make Sequencing Cards

Create some sequencing cards with photographs and a brief story about several activities you have observed. Review these at a group meeting and then leave them out for the children to use.

Use Audio or Video for Immediate Review

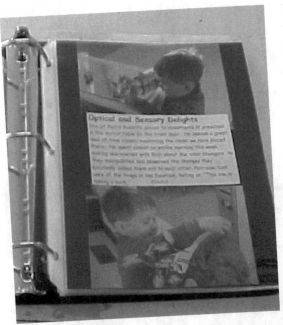

Use an audio or video tape or a digital camera with a display screen that allows the children to immediately revisit what they have just been doing. Take observation notes on what they say and do in response and bring this back to them the next day.

Alternatively, audio-tape a play segment and transcribe it to be read to the children. Ask if they would like to do anything more with this idea. Record their discussion about this possibility and bring it back to them the next day.

Make a Theme Book

Choose a focus for gathering some observations about a childhood theme the children have been exploring, for instance, sensory play, friendships and conflict, or family life, and create a book with different children pursuing each theme. Read this to the children and put it in the book area for regular use.

Observations Can Enhance Partnerships with Coworkers and Families

Your documentation not only serves as an accountability system for your teaching, it has great potential to contribute to the formation of strong partnerships with your coworkers and the children's families. While working closely with parents is an emphasis in our professional literature, our busy lives and potential communication barriers often leave this ideal of partnerships as a vague abstraction or an unmet goal.

Partnerships develop over time and most effectively occur when there is mutual respect and something specific to focus on. When you are generous with your observations, revealing how you value the details of what the children are doing and how carefully you think through your planning for them, parents will be eager to add their knowledge and stay in close communication.

Ann Pelo describes how she uses her observations with families in this way:

> *Stories, photos, and detailed notes invite families to join teachers in thinking about what's happening with their children. Working in full-day child care, I don't see parents every day; actually, there are some parents whom I rarely see because our schedules don't intersect at all. But parents come to the classroom every day, whether I see them or not, and they look around and try to get glimpses of what their children are doing.*

When teachers conscientiously design and display observation stories for parents, they get more respect and involvement from them. This, in turn, begins to transform teachers' own attitudes and communications. You become more curious, less judgmental, and willing to go that extra mile to make it possible for the children's families to be involved with what you are doing.

Publicly sharing your observations can enhance your teamwork as a staff too. Often schedules in full-day children's programs make it difficult for the morning and afternoon staff to meet and plan together daily. You can post some observation notes including your questions or thinking and invite other teachers to add theirs. Even with minimal overlap in your schedules, this will help you work more closely with a similar focus. It is also a way to informally mentor new or less experienced teachers to observe, think about, and communicate what they are seeing and hearing.

Take Another Look

Because your observation stories are such an important tool for learning to collaborate, it makes sense to invent some systems to share them with the children's families and your coworkers. Here are some strategies to try.

Create a Parent Notice Board

Designate a particular area of the room for posting things for parents. Find at least three different ways to alert them to this posting, for instance, a note in newsletters, cubbies, or on the door; phone calls, e-mails, or a tour at drop-off or pickup time; colorful paper footprints from the entryway to the board. Include a clipboard or notepad in your posting for getting immediate input from families.

Send Home an Observation Book

Develop a traveling notebook binder with observation notes and photos in plastic sleeves and set up a check out system for this to go home with the children. Make its language child-friendly so that it can become a family reading project. Include a blank page for families to add a response to their reading.

Ask for Family Discussion Pages

Send home a short page of questions or discussion prompts for the family to fill out together and be added as a page for your book on "family discussions about what we do in the children's program." Topics might include ordinary moments, such as "how we see people becoming friends" or something about a particular project focus such as "learning about life in a wheelchair." See pages 112–113 for examples of forms you could adapt for this purpose.

Use Computers to Share Observations

If most of your parent population has access to e-mail, send a quick observation story with photos to them at work or at home. Invite them to send a response. Print all of these and put them in a notebook binder on the sign-in desk, hall, or entryway table.

If you have the technology and software such as PowerPoint or PhotoDelux, run a computer display of an observation story in your entryway. You could also do this with a VCR if you are gathering observations with a video camera.

Create a Staff Observation Sharing System

Designate a place for sharing observations with your coworkers, making sure it is set up for two-way communication. Agree on a system for keeping current with how you are making use of this. When you invent a system that works well for you, share it with other teachers, in your program, and in the profession at large through an Internet discussion group, a conference presentation, or writing for a professional newsletter, magazine, or journal.

As you work with observation at the heart of your teaching, you will discover all the ways it can be used to enhance your goals and even provoke new ones. Mindful observing is a give-and-take cyclical process. You will also find great enjoyment and benefit in reading stories of other teachers who demonstrate the various ways you can practice being a teacher-researcher, putting your observations of children at the center of your thinking, storytelling, and advocacy for getting the resources you need to do this kind of work.

Recommended Resources

Curtis, D., and M. Carter. *Reflecting Children's Lives. A Handbook for Planning Child Centered Curriculum.* St Paul: Redleaf Press, 1996. This is a valuable text for setting up your environment and curriculum approach so that they reflect the time of childhood and the specific children in your program.

Diffily, D., and K. Morrison, eds. *Family Friendly Communications for Early Childhood Programs.* Washington, D.C.: NAEYC, 1996. This book offers descriptive paragraphs of what children learn as they play with the idea that teachers will copy these for use in their communications with families.

Gallas, K. *Talking Their Way into Science. Hearing Children's Questions and Theories, Responding with Curricula.* New York: Teachers College Press, 1995. The author gives us a firsthand look at how teaching can be more successful when it is built on children's questions and ideas.

Paley, V. *Wally's Stories. Conversations in the Kindergarten.* Cambridge, MA: Harvard University Press, 1981. This is basic reading for anyone who wants to learn how the author developed her curriculum around hearing the children's stories.

———. *The Girl with the Brown Crayon.* Cambridge, MA: Harvard University Press, 1997. In this book we see how a teacher reexamines her own understandings by observing and listening carefully to her kindergartners.

Pelo, A., and F. Davidson. *That's Not Fair! A Teacher's Guild to Activism with Young Children.* St. Paul: Redleaf Press, 2000. This book offers a practical and inspiring look at how observations of children's interests and values of social justice can be integrated into a child-centered anti-bias curriculum approach.

Reynolds, G., and E. Jones. *Master Players. Learning from Children at Play.* New York: Teachers College Press, 1997. The detailed observations of this book are instructive for anyone who wants to enhance their understanding and appreciation of the meaning of children's socio-dramatic play. There is also a valuable chapter from Elizabeth Prescott outlining her teaching of the art of observation.

12

Getting Organized to Make Childhood Valued

Through close observation of and personal relationship with each child and with the life of the classroom, one develops a sense of which moments to try to capture. Because I know, for example, that Elise has been engaging mostly in solitary play, I will take special note when she offers a spare Lego piece to Frank. Or because I know that Toshi and Jami have been talking endlessly about huge giants, I will take a picture when they begin to build tall block structures together. The observing and recording that a teacher does in an emergent context is not based on developmental checklists or assessment portfolios—it is a manifestation of her active engagement with the life of the program, and with the children.

Sarah Felstiner

As a teacher, nourishing your disposition and skills for observing is critical to enjoying and being successful in your job. With this foundation, you will come to appreciate who children are and find yourself eager to awaken others to the contribution these young ones can make to our lives. But none of this will come to pass without some planning and tools to make your observations visible. You will need to get organized for this to be central to your work as a teacher.

Organizing systems will vary from person to person and program to program, according to your individual style, program expectations, and working conditions. You will want to consider your own preferences, your work environment, and the tools and technology you have available. This chapter summarizes ways to get yourself, your documentation, and your colleagues organized to teach with a bigger vision for childhood and our culture.

Adopt a Method That Suits Your Style

The most important thing is to get started observing the children you work with. Choose a way of taking notes that suits your personal style as a teacher. For example, if you are not a particularly methodical person, you might start your observing practice in one of two ways: Put either paper or sticky notes with pens in containers that are easy to reach all around your room. Some teachers find it helpful to wear an apron with a front pocket containing these things; others keep handy a simple spiral notebook with a pen attached. If you adopt one of these methods, you will have taken the first step toward writing notes about what you see and hear.

Once you begin regularly writing down quick observation notes, you will then need a system for organizing the data you collect. Some teachers set up individual folders or journals for each child and drop their notes into these. This works well for observing individual children, but doesn't provide a system for observations that include groups of children. You will need an additional sorting file for that data. Many teachers create group files and then make photocopies for each child file or portfolio. However you choose to handle this, it is important that you have a way of tracking observations with interactions between children, their conversations, conflicts, or growing common interests. This will enable you to discover their patterns, passions, and possible curriculum themes to pursue.

If you prefer efficient organizational schemes, you might set up a bulletin board display with brief descriptions of the learning teachers plan for. Under each description put a clear plastic sleeve or stand where you can insert written notes and photos of your observations of children's learning. You can find descriptions of the categories in any number of professional resources (for example, *The Portfolio and Its Use, Book II: A Road Map for Assessment* by Sharon MacDonald—Little Rock, AR, Southern Early Childhood Association, 1996—or *The High Scope K–3 Curriculum*—Ypsilanti, MI, High Scope Foundation, 1990), or you can create your own in simple, child-friendly language. Creating a visible system for sorting and displaying your notes and photos demonstrates that you are carefully watching and thinking about what is unfolding with the children in your room. This is really the intent behind requirements for teachers to display curriculum plans and do portfolio assessments. Each week you can move your posted documentation into individual children's portfolios, making duplicate copies where more than one child is involved.

If this open-ended approach seems difficult for you, consider using predesigned forms. There are a number of these available commercially, but most are focused on assessing growth and development without attention to the full range of what is unfolding with the children. If you want to use forms, consider inventing ones that focus on the broad topics of the earlier study sessions of this book. This will keep you alert to the details of children's actions and conversations and allow you to build on your notes to tell others the story and meaning of what was observed. Here are some simple examples based on the themes explored in this book:

Topic: Friendships and Conflicts   Date ____/____/____ Time _____

Observed/Heard:_____

_____

Significance of this event: _____

_____

Topic: Power and Adventure   Date ____/____/____ Time _____

Observed/Heard:_____

_____

Significance of this event: _____

_____

Topic: Literacy and Symbolic Representation   Date ____/____/____ Time _____

Observed/Heard:_____

_____

Significance of this event: _____

_____

Whatever your preference, choose an initial system that will get you right into the process of observing and organizing your data. Over time you may want to refine or change it, but the goal is to get started and hurdle any initial barriers that may be in your way. If you work in a program that has specific forms or paperwork systems required for assessments or accountability, your challenge is to reduce, not expand, any duplication of effort. You will have to experiment with how to integrate the anecdotal visual story approach into your requirements. If you do this well, you will have evidence of your accountability and can begin to lobby for a more streamlined system that suits your needs.

Keep Observations Simple and Short

The typical early childhood teacher is responsible for a large group of children, along with many housekeeping and paperwork tasks. If you think that collecting observations will require a large block of time to just sit and watch, weeks will slip by without you recording anything. Yet when you take five to ten minutes to jot down something you saw or heard, because it delighted or irritated you, provoked your curiosity, or seemed significant, you will soon find yourself with a collection of small observations that can be strung together, like beads on a string.

The idea of seeing observations as beads on a string comes from college teacher Elizabeth Prescott. She uses the metaphor of beads to stand for children's activities, with the spaces in between representing transitions. You can also think of the spaces between these beads as the passage of time. If you approach the observation process with this metaphor of collecting beads on a string, you will find a rhythm that looks like this: As you move about the room, you notice when a child or group of children begins to play or engage in something that is likely to last for a while. Jotting down some details is a potential bead for your string. When the activity ends or the children start to shift their attention to other things, this is a stopping place for this particular observation, a space on the string. Over time, as you continue this process and look over the notes and photos you have collected, you will notice which beads make sense to string together to tell a story of what has been going on with this child or group of children.

In teaching you how to record what you see, most observation textbooks make distinctions among a number of techniques:

- Running records
- Time samplings
- Event samplings
- Checklists
- Anecdotal records
- Diary or journal descriptions

The typical teacher rarely has time to employ all of these techniques. Prescott suggests trying an adaptation of running records, using lined paper and describing each new action of a child on a separate line. This enables you to notice closely, while quickly writing words or phrases. In the busy life of a classroom, you will probably want to invent word abbreviations for yourself. Whether you use a clipboard with lined paper, a form, or a small sticky-note pad, the point is to jot down enough details to jog your memory when you find time to return to fill in more complete anecdotal information. With practice you will begin to develop a rhythm for yourself, knowing when to just watch and not write, and when to lower your eyes and concentrate on a moment of writing.

Consider Your Work Environment

Hand in hand with considerations of your own personal style are considerations of your work environment. Are you teaching alone or as part of a team? Do you have paid planning time that can be used for analyzing and developing stories from your observation data? Are there resources and support to help you with any languages or cross-cultural aspects of understanding the meaning of your observations? Do you have work space and the tools that you need to create visual stories with your documentation?

Programs vary greatly in these areas. To teach with the pedagogy this book suggests, the ideal working conditions include the following:

- Paid time to study and create displays of your documentation
- Opportunities for collaborative discussions with other teachers
- Resources on child development and the specific cultural and linguistic makeup of children and their families
- Basic technology, including a camera and tape recorder for your room, and a copy machine, computer, scanner, and printer in a work space away from the children
- A budget for film, developing, color copying, or color ink cartridges and photo-quality paper for your printer
- Basic training on the use of helpful technology, visual art materials, and the elements of graphic design, and further writing or second language skills you may need

If you looked at that list and panicked, fear not. Don't let the lack of something on the list keep you from beginning to observe the children you work with. Everything on this list is achievable, if not available at the moment. Together with your coworkers and director, you can begin to prioritize these as goals for your program. If your program is nonprofit, grants can be written for most of the items on this list. Most programs have parents who are willing to donate small things like film and notebook binders; some include them on the initial list of things to bring at the time of enrollment, along with immunization records, comfort toys for nap time, and the like. Often parents have employers or connections with people who have resources they would be willing to donate in the areas of technology and training. You can put out a request for ideas on many of the on-line early childhood discussion groups. Find examples of how other programs have scheduled time for collaboration and working on documentation. Here are some suggestions from teacher Ann Pelo.

If you teach alone

- Find another teacher in your program who will be your observation partner. You may be able to spend time in each other's classrooms. For example, while your kids are in music class, you can visit each other's classrooms. Whether or not you spend time in each other's rooms, you can share notes, sketches, and photos of children and talk together about the children's growth and learning.
- Invite parents to spend time in your classroom. You can ask a parent to be available to children when they need help, so that you can spend some time observing, or you can ask a parent to observe and take notes for you while you work with children. If you ask parents to spend time observing, it's helpful to be specific with them about what you'd like the focus of the observations to be.
- On a bulletin board in the teacher lounge or in the office, post some notes that you took while observing kids and ask other teachers to jot down their thoughts and insights about what you observed.
- Include time on the agenda of staff meetings to talk about observations of children. Teachers on your staff can take turns bringing notes, sketches, or photos to the staff meeting for teachers to discuss together.

If you teach in a team

- Schedule some time each week with your co-teacher when one of you will spend time observing children while the other teacher keeps track of general classroom activity.
- Develop cues to use with each other that signal that "I want to step out of the action and watch this play for a few minutes." Be sure to wait for an okay from your co-teacher before you move into observation mode.
- Schedule a regular time to talk with your co-teacher about your observations. Some teachers use naptime to talk together; others set up regular meetings with their co-teachers about what they observe.

Getting started

- Schedule fifteen minutes for observation at a time during the day when the children are typically engaged in play. Write it on your daily schedule to honor your plan to observe children.
- Choose one area of the room to observe. What are kids doing in the block area? How are they using playdough?
- Focus on a particular child; watch and listen to her play, taking notes and photos.

- Pose a question that you are curious about and pursue that question with observations. "How do children use books in my classroom?" "Do girls and boys use the blocks in different or similar ways?" "What role does Keiko, our youngest child, play in our group?"

Consider Other Tools for Gathering Documentation

Along with your observation notes, other pieces of data will be useful to help you fill in the details of what has unfolded. Sketches, photos, audio or video tape recordings, examples of things children have made, and additional resources you have offered all serve to help you remember, analyze, develop hunches, and then translate this into a meaningful story.

Audiotapes

There are some occasions, such as a focused group time, when you can be sure a tape recorder will help you capture conversation that goes by faster than you can write down. Using a tape recorder doesn't oblige you to transcribe everything you record. Rather, it serves as a backup for your documentation process and gives you the option of listening or transcribing to meet your needs. As a teacher new to observing and documenting, you may find a tape recorder a valuable addition to your own eyes and ears. Listening to tapes and comparing them with your notes or memory can help you find things you missed. Audiotapes from your classroom can become your teacher.

It's easy to overdo audio recording and then never find time to listen to or transcribe the tapes. Be selective, primarily using a tape recorder for occasions when you want backup insurance. Many teachers choose to use only one tape, recording with it over and over. This forces them to immediately transcribe anything they want to preserve, rather than building up a stack of tapes waiting to be heard or transcribed.

As technology advances and audio recorders become more integrated with computers and multiple-voice-recognition software, the job of transcribing tapes will become automated and thus much less time consuming. Imagine the ease of inserting an audio disk from your recorder into your computer and having it immediately translate it into printable words! In the meantime, you may find someone who can donate the old technology of a foot pedal to turn the tape recorder on and off as you transcribe. Headphones are also helpful in listening to or transcribing tapes.

Photographs and Videotapes

Having a camera handy is very useful for documentation. You can take photos of the children, processes they are engaged in, and things they have created. Close-up, still photos are important companions to your notes. They will often help you see something you neglected to record. It is a bit more complicated to use a video camera, take notes, and still be responsible for a group of children. Some teachers use volunteers for this purpose, while others mount a video camera on a tripod and focus in on a particular set of materials or part of the room children may move to and from. With the rapid advancement of technology, digital still and video cameras, it will soon be possible for one camera to meet most of your needs. In the meantime, here are some options to consider:

- **Polaroid instant cameras:** While these have the advantage of generating an immediate print, overall these cameras don't allow you to get close-up, detailed pictures. The film is comparatively expensive, not standard from camera to camera, and not always available at your nearest store.

- **Disposable cameras:** These are sturdy, easy to use, and often a good choice for early childhood programs. Teachers can quickly place a number of cameras throughout the center. They can even be sent home for photos to be taken with the children's families. Overall they are more expensive, however, and the photos are of a lesser quality than a sturdy 35-millimeter "point and shoot" camera.

- **35-millimeter automated cameras:** The price on these cameras makes them fairly affordable and the zoom lens option allows you to capture close-up images of children and their work, as well as group shots. Most camera shops recommend 400-speed ASA film for capturing faster-moving subjects, such

as children at play. Buying film in bulk keeps costs down, but you still need an organized system for purchasing and developing film in a timely fashion. Who will be responsible for dropping off and picking up film? How often will film be developed? For photos to be of much use in accompanying observation notes, they need to be developed quickly.

- **Digital camera:** Whether still or video, digital cameras can save time and money, eliminating the cost of film and developing, and allow you to immediately share them on the screen, or as prints from a color printer. Increasingly digital cameras are made to plug directly into your printer for quick copies, or you can use them with computer software that allows you to capture a still photo from a video and combine any of your images with text. At the time of this writing, digital cameras are still expensive, but the price is steadily coming down. You need a quality color printer and more expensive photo print paper to produce images similar in quality to traditional photo developing.

Technology is advancing rapidly in today's world and the good news is that it is becoming more affordable and user friendly. Recommendations on particular products would be out of date before you read them here. When you are ready to research or purchase equipment, you can readily access on-line or print consumer reports that compare options within your price range, such as the Web site at www.cnet.com.

Here are some guidelines to keep in mind as you begin to purchase technology to help you gather and display documentation.

- Consider your use and space. Copy machines, computers, printers, and scanners need to be located away from the children but accessible to them at particular times. You will want them available when teachers are available, not tied up by office staff or located in a frequently used conference space. There needs to be plenty of work space nearby, as well as storage for an ample supply of paper, toner, disks, ink cartridges, user manuals, and related guides. Lighting and ventilation are also considerations. All of these factors will influence the size and amount of the equipment you can reasonably use.

- Consider durability, maintenance, and ease of use. One of the most important factors in choosing technology for early childhood programs is how well it can handle multiple users. People with varying amounts of knowledge and skill need to find the equipment user friendly. It shouldn't require complicated steps or finicky maintenance.

- Consider your technical know-how and basic needs. All the bells and whistles of advancing technology are impressive and seductive, but will they be easy to use by the typical teacher? You will need some initial training and technical assistance, often available from a parent or nearby business, so that all staff members feel equally able to make use of the technology. After that, your program will want to be fairly self-reliant in using and problem-solving with the technology you use, so avoid purchasing anything too complicated in its basic use. Photocopiers should have an enlarging and reducing feature. With cameras you need to be able to quickly capture sharp images of active children. This means a fast shutter speed, battery charge, and zoom lens.

To capture sound, you need video or tape recorders with wide-ranging microphones. An extra supply of long-running batteries and a charger are a must. Any equipment that will be used around children must be able to withstand the impact of their unpredictable actions.

- Consider software that will aid your visual displays. Software is developing as rapidly as hardware, and you can find a number of products that will help you create attractive visual presentations. These include a range of printable fonts, graphic layout elements, and photo manipulation features. A word of caution: All fonts and graphic elements need to be simple enough to highlight, not detract from, the real message of the story. Also, some programs are in a position to send images and observation stories to parents via e-mail or by posting them on their own Web site. This may sound attractive, but it involves extra time and training for the teachers, who need paid time within their workday to make this a viable option.

- Consider traditional art supplies as your friends. As valuable as some of the technology can be for teachers, you will want to have some basic office and art supplies at your fingertips. These include sticky-note pads, three-ring notebook binders, and plastic sleeves; hole punch, X-Acto knives, paper cutters, and high-quality scissors; a cutting board, fine ruler, triangle, and T-square; basic black and white cardstock paper, along with a small selection of specialty papers; foam core and mat board (often donated as scrap from frame shops); a variety of adhesives, from glue sticks to paste and Velcro. Special note: If you want your documentation preserved long term, consider acid-free adhesives and papers.

However basic or advanced your tools, keep in mind that they are a means to making your observations visible, not an end in themselves. Your personal working style and program considerations will determine the best documentation system for you, while you strive to be as cost- and time-efficient as possible. Once you have developed a method of gathering observation notes and related visuals, your task will be to make it visible as a story to capture people's attention: the children, their families, your coworkers, and visitors to your program.

Recommended Resources

Creating Better Child Care Jobs. Model Work Standards for Teaching Staff in Center-Based Child Care. Washington, D.C.: Center for the Child Care Work Force, 1998. Set up in a similar self-study format as the NAEYC accreditation process, this booklet offers criteria for thirteen components of a work environment that enables early childhood teachers to do their jobs well.

Jablon, J., A. Dombro, and M. Dichtelmiller. *The Power of Observation.* Washington, D.C.: Teaching Strategies Inc., 1999. This is a user-friendly book outlining the basics of observation skills and techniques.

Lawrence, I. *Gotta Minute? Quick Tips for Getting Organized.* New York: Robert D. Reed, 2000. Though not focused on the life of a teacher, the tips offered in this book can be translated to help you make better use of your time and materials.

Leonard, A. *I Spy Something. A Practical Guide to Classroom Observations of Young Children.* Little Rock, Arkansas: Southern Early Childhood Association, 1997. This guide offers some of the traditional approaches to early childhood education, with a human face and practical strategies.

Schlenger, S., and R. Roesch. *How to Be Organized in Spite of Yourself.* New York: Signet, 1999. There are a number of strategies in this book that teachers could adapt for organizing the array of tasks and paperwork that are part of their work.

Making Observations Visible

13

As we move around the circle of life, there are certain things we must do if we are to learn and grow and live a good life. The first step is to listen. If we do not listen, then we will hear nothing. The second step is to observe. If we do not look carefully at things, then we will not really see them. The third step is to remember. If we do not remember those things we have learned, then we have learned nothing. The fourth step is to share. If we do not share, then the circle does not continue.

Joseph Bruchac

Becoming an aware listener and observer will surely enhance your view of children, and it has the potential to enhance others' view of children as well. In the early childhood field, writing up observations is usually approached as an assessment task or a requirement imposed by supervisors. This often has teachers viewing children with a particular focus or a checklist to be completed. While there are valuable uses for this kind of data collection, the process and form it takes tends to have a clinical, rather than human, quality to it. More often than not, when the write-up leaves the teacher's hands, it ends up in a forgotten file or on the floor of a parent's car. The effort the teacher has made in these situations leaves no one particularly thoughtful or eager for more.

Making our observations visible could have a more powerful impact on everyone if we approach the task as a process of collecting and telling the stories of the remarkable experiences of childhood. When teachers turn their observations into oral, written, and visual stories, children sense that their pursuits are worthy of being documented, described, and remembered. Their families, too, are rewarded with the details of what the children have been doing, thinking, and learning. And teachers get windows into how their coworkers think, what they find as significant and meaningful.

Here's how preschool teacher Ann Pelo describes this process of making her observations visible:

> To provide windows into children's play and learning for families, I try to create bulletin boards which reflect the evolving life of the children, with photos and quotes from kids and examples of the work they are doing as a project unfolds. These windows invite families to look at children's play with curiosity and delight.
>
> If I'm there when parents are dropping off or picking up their children, I try to lure them over to a bulletin board, to point out details: "I took that photo when we first began using a wheelchair in our classroom. Kids noticed right away that our shelves were too low for them to reach if they sat in a wheelchair, and they began talking about how to make our classroom more fair."
>
> Lately, I've tried to include brief statements about my thinking in displays, so that even if I'm not there, I can "talk" with parents. I might add a question that helped guide my planning or pose a question for viewers to consider. I might add tips for parents to use as they study their children's work. I write things like:
>
> "I wasn't sure how much the children understood about using a wheelchair. I took these notes while they took turns riding in a wheelchair, so I could learn more about what they understood."
>
> "What are your goals for your child as she or he investigates accessibility issues and ramps?"
>
> "Notice the different ways that the children tried to draw the depth of a ramp. It's a challenge to move from three dimensions into two."

Finding the Story Worth Telling

Once you become a keen observer you discover that each day holds dozens of stories that could be told. There is neither time nor space for all of these to be shared, so your task becomes one of selecting and highlighting what you think needs public recognition, what can be told verbally to the children, which story lends itself well to a visual display, or which can be a simple sound bite to include in a child's journal or portfolio.

Finding the story worth telling depends on a number of factors, including the message you want to convey and the audience you are trying to reach.

Stories to Give Back to Children

Children benefit from having their own activities told back to them as oral and visual stories. This needs to be timely and in child-friendly language. Perhaps you want to give recognition for an effort or accomplishment of an individual or group of children. Or you may choose an observation, some quotes, and visuals that represent some activity you think has the potential to grow into a long-term project. The very act of making it visible to the children will likely sustain their interest and encourage them to pursue further aspects.

On other occasions, you may want to highlight for the whole group some individual or small cluster activity, perhaps something you value or have been trying to promote among the children, such as a way to work through a conflict, solve a problem, approach a task, or learn a skill. This public recognition helps the children see each other as a resource for their learning, come to value what each other is doing and thinking, and feel part of the overall group.

Stories for Coworkers and Children's Families

Another reason you may choose to make an observation visible is because it highlights something you have been puzzled about or eager for some dialogue around with your coworkers and the children's families. Perhaps this has to do with something controversial such as the amount of play or direct instruction needed for school readiness; or how much intervention is required in children's conflicts, expressions of bias, or play that involves violence or superhero play. You may want to make visible a transcript of some children's conversation and how you are thinking about it, inviting others to add their thoughts.

Here's an example of a story from Sarah Felstiner, encouraging dialogue about Power Ranger play by making her observations and thoughts publicly visible by posting this on the bulletin board:

Sunlight Group teachers have noticed lots of "Power Ranger" play, and we've heard from some families that children are playing about Power Rangers at home too. We've been talking at our weekly team meeting about how to address this obvious need some children have to play out the action stories they see on television. Is this their way of physically and emotionally processing the intense input of a show like Power Rangers? *Is it safe for children? Is it comfortable for grownups? What kind of support or intervention, if any, should we as teachers offer?*

Our first step in answering these questions has been to stick close to that play when it's happening, in order to ensure all children's physical safety, and to observe more closely the play that's going on. What specific elements of the Power Rangers *show do children play about? What developmental needs underlie this play? What questions are children asking through their play?*

Here's a transcript of one morning's worth of Power Ranger play between Max, Ben, and Glenn that took place in the drama area. (We also have seen Power Ranger play at gym time, at the park, and in the building area). In this game, I tried to intervene as little as possible, offering guidelines only when it seemed to be a safety issue.

Max: "I'm the green ranger!"
Ben: "I'm the gold ranger!"
Glenn: "I'm the silver ranger!"

They each take a sequined elastic headband from the dress up pegs and begin flinging them like slingshots, mostly up in the air and at the mirror. I ask them to be careful not to hit me, or any other children, and to keep their headband game inside the drama area.

Ben: "We're fighting the Sonics!"

Glenn: "Oh boy, we're destroying the power lines."

Their headbands are going farther afield now, often hitting the hanging decorations and other things in the drama space. I tell them that I'm concerned, and Ben shows me how they can still spring their headbands without letting go, so I agree. Max points his headband at Muriel and flings it toward her, still holding on. I tell him that he can play this with the kids in his game, but I won't let him shoot them at other kids.

Glenn: "We're in our spaceship."

They begin scooting and rolling the big log on the floor, in order to bring it farther into the drama area and into their game.

Ben: "Silver Ranger, what's up?"

Max: (holding a wicker basket full of small stones): "These are cycles. Cycle-rangers."

Ben: "Silver Ranger, I got the treasure we wanted."

Glenn: (holding a basket of rocks and shells): "Okay, I'm gonna X-ray all of this—turn it into bombs."

The game is sidetracked momentarily by a disagreement over who had which sparkly headband. They both look blue to me, but after some careful checking the boys sort it out. Now all the boys have climbed onto the large log and are using it as a "helicopter."

Ben: "I'm on the computer."

They get out a basket of small tiles and begin arranging them on top of the log.

Ben: "This is the power line. We're blowing up those houses."

Glenn: "We need to go to bomb-dot-com."

Ben: "Thanks for turning those into bombs." (He adds a carpet square). "Look at this power bomb."

Max (getting a basket of nuts): "Look at these power bombs."

Ben: "This whole log is gonna blast into pieces."

Glenn: "I sure made a lot of bombs."

Ben: "You sure made us do hard work."

They all continue carefully laying out materials on the log, balancing them and arranging them, working in silence.

Ben: "I'm Tommy."

Max: "I'm Tommy."

Ben: "We're both Tommy."

Max: "Yup."

Glenn: "Okay, you guys, we're gonna blow up the power lines."

Max: "I'll count to ten. One, two, three …"

Glenn: "Hey, wait! I'm not done."

Max: "I'm not playing."

Glenn: "You have to clean up only what you played with. Actually, I'm cleaning up too."

Ben: "Me too. Let's put everything away."

All three boys make continual explosion noises as they sort their materials and place them back in the wicker baskets on the shelf of the drama area. Watching the boys play, I found myself glad to see them using the unstructured natural materials available in the drama area. In many preschools, spaces for dramatic play are stocked with sinks and stoves and dishes and dolls, defining the space as a place to play "house." For that reason, drama and dress up play is often the domain of the girls. Our drama space is more welcoming to boys, I think, because its openness and flexibility invites a wider variety of play. I was also pleased to see the boys doing some negotiation and problem-solving work. Dramatic play is rich with opportunities for conflict resolution and alternate perspective–taking, and some of that came through in this game. Perhaps as we do more observation of children's Power Ranger play, we can begin to talk with them, and with families, about ways to meet the needs and pursue the interests that their play expresses, while sustaining a safe and peaceful classroom environment.

Topics such as superhero play are complex and require extensive observation and dialogue among the adults in order to respond to the underlying developmental themes the children are pursuing. As a result of their sharpening observation skills and adult communication systems, Felstiner and her colleagues were able to have more meaningful discussions among themselves and with the children's parents, exploring ways to handle the controversial issue of kids acting out scenes that included shooting and blowing things up. This allowed them to rally around some common goals, even though they had different perspectives on the value of this play. Investigation replaced the knee-jerk reactions and polarization of opinions of years past. Both the teachers and the parents felt respected for their concerns, and they all felt they benefited from the dialogue that carried on for many weeks.

Stories to Become Our History Books

If we want children to remember and cherish their time in our programs, collecting stories of their significant experiences with us can become our history or memory books. Keeping alive these memories in book form will simultaneously promote literacy and enduring shared experiences. These books need to go beyond a scrapbook or photo album format and have details told with engaging language, the children's and yours.

Writing Helps You Find, As Well As Tell, a Story

With a combination of photos, children's words or work samples, and even sketchy observation notes you can often discover a story worth developing and telling. The challenge is to find the words that will engage the reader and convey the meaning you hope they will discover in your story. Though there is a saying that a picture is worth a thousand words, you should use photographs to help you generate descriptive words, not as a substitute for them. Consider the difference between a photo caption and a descriptive story used with photos.

CAPTION	DESCRIPTIVE STORY
Everybody had fun at the pumpkin farm, especially Tina.	Once we arrived at the pumpkin farm, everyone burst onto the field, arms outstretched as if to embrace each ball of orange. Tina bent down closely to look at each one, perhaps picturing its soon-to-be-face.

Learning some strategies to help you find the descriptive words to bring your story alive, with or without photos, will help you make your observations visible.

Practice Using Word Webs to Generate Descriptive Details

In chapter 8 you practiced an Art of Awareness activity where you created a word web. You can use this simple strategy to begin to spin out words for your observation story. Put a single word or a photo in the center of a piece of paper and then from this draw out other words, particularly action verbs and sensory adjectives and adverbs that could be used to describe more about this idea. Make a goal of generating at least ten initial words. Then try to find three other words to spin off from each of the ten. Now you have the bones of a good story.

Choose the words that seem most appropriate and appealing to you and begin to form them into short sentences. Soon you will have a few sentences to make up a descriptive paragraph, like the simple descriptive story above about the pumpkin farm. If you have them, you can also insert actual quotes from the children themselves, either from when they were involved in the activity, or when you showed them a photo of it.

Practice Collaborative Webbing and Writing

Working with others to develop stories is a great way to expand your perspectives as well as your vocabulary of descriptive words. Collaborative word webbing helps you mentor each other across your areas of strengths and learning goals. Some teachers become keen observers but are hesitant in their writing skills. Others find that words flow easily in oral storytelling, but they need a scribe to translate their ideas into print. Before working on your observation notes together, try practicing this activity with another person.

1. One person should be the storyteller, while the other is the scribe.
2. The storyteller should begin describing a favorite memory of a time working with a child. Describe as many sensory details as possible. What was the time

of year, the temperature of the day, the lighting, sounds, and smells? What specifically unfolded when you were together? Are there facial expressions, colors, or actions you can describe in detail?

3. While the storyteller is talking, the scribe creates a web of words and phrases from the story.

4. Before you change roles, the scribe should add some additional words that come to mind from the story, putting them on a different place on the web.

5. Change roles with the scribe becoming the storyteller and the first storyteller becoming the scribe. Following the same guidelines, repeat the activity in your new roles.

6. When both people have told their stories, exchange the word webs, so that you each have words for your own stories in front of you. Take these words and begin to write a paragraph of your story.

The next time you work together, you can practice with actual observation notes and photos of children in your care.

Practice Writing from Three Perspectives

Typically observations are written up with a focus on some aspect of the learning or development seen in a child's activity. While this is valuable, it is only one of the possible stories you could be telling. If we want to make children's lives visible and valued, it is important to tell stories that capture an activity from their point of view, not only those with an adult agenda. This requires looking closely at the details and trying to discover how the child might be experiencing what is happening. Questions to help you find this perspective are listed in the chart below.

The learning and development story is one teachers are typically most at ease in telling. This is where we draw upon our professional resources and goals for children. We can interpret what we see happening in light of our understandings of ages and stages, how children learn, and the developmental process of acquiring dispositions, knowledge, and skills. This is the story parents and teachers are usually most eager to see because it reflects the outcomes of our work. When you are writing from this perspective, use the questions below to guide your thinking.

As the teacher, you, too, have a perspective that is important for others to hear. Not only do others benefit from the detailed stories of what is going on for the child, but it is worthwhile for them to hear how you are thinking about this observation. What questions, meaning, and planning ideas does this observation leave you with? Hearing your perspectives on this will serve as a model for others as they consider observation descriptions and analyze photos and samples of children's work. They will learn what you value and how you go about developing plans and goals for children. Your story is a wonderful window into the heart and mind of a teacher.

THE CHILD'S STORY	THE LEARNING AND DEVELOPMENT STORY	THE TEACHER'S STORY
• What is the child doing with the material or object? • What seems to be engaging about it? • How does the child talk about and represent her thinking in her play? • What other experiences, people, and materials does she connect with it? • What is she inventing and investigating through this play or activity?	• How does this activity relate to things you've seen before or heard about from the child's family? • What new ideas, questions, understandings or solutions, is the child coming up with? • Is there any confusion, contradiction, stereotype, or misinformation coming out in this activity? • How is this experience supporting or undermining a positive sense of identity for this child? • What do professional resources add to your understanding?	• What were you delighted with or bothered by in this activity? How does this experience fit with what you value? • How does what you see fit with what you already know about this child or group? • What are you curious about? • What do you want to know more about? • What hunches do you have about the meaning of this activity for this child or for these children? What speculations or predictions do you want to explore? • What are possible next steps you can take to support or challenge the play and learning here?

You can practice writing from each of these perspectives with each set of notes and documentation collections you gather. Working alone or as a team, you can also practice by viewing a short video clip of a child or small group of children engaged in some self-directed activity. Use the questions above to help you develop a list of phrases or word webs that can be developed into sentences and a paragraph representing each perspective.

Writing from the first column takes the child's point of view and should be full of active, sensory words that fill out your understandings of what this experience was like from within that young body. Choose quotes and observation details from your notes and expand them with words and phrases that vividly express the meaning or theme of this experience from the child's perspective.

For the second column study your observation data and take into account the words from the child's perspective in the first column. For assistance, you can draw on your developmental charts or resource materials to find the professional language of assessing learning and development. Or you can use your own phrases that describe the growth and learning you see.

As you write from your word list or web in the third column, try to speak with your own voice as you describe what's on your mind when you study your observation—your questions, curiosities, hunches, and possible plans. Here you reveal yourself as researcher, meaning maker, relationship builder, and curriculum planner.

If you are writing collaboratively, each of you can develop a story for one of the columns. Or, time permitting, each team can write stories from all three perspectives so that you can learn from each others' approach. Working this way helps you learn to collaborate, expand your storytelling repertoire, your vocabulary, and your ability to turn observations into lively sentences and paragraphs.

Observation notes:

7/23 Coe using bead rack again; put Jeanne's hand on beads; watched her making sound; imitated her brrrruuuum sound

7/30 Coe took camera from Jeanne, held to face, tipped head back, made whirring sound, tapped on back of camera

CHILD'S STORY	LEARNING AND DEVELOPMENT STORY	TEACHER'S STORY
• Watching closely, especially connecting with sounds • Using distinct sounds "brrrrrruuum" "whirrrrrrrr" • Inviting playmate • Pleased to get message across	• Using gestures and sounds to communicate • Accurately imitating • Showing social skill • Fine motor skills • Cause and Effect • Displaying confidence, pleased with results	• Amazed at ability to get his message across • Will words replace this expanded creativity in communication? • Will he transfer these sounds to similar materials? • Is the sound as interesting to him as the object itself? • What other ways does he try to engage others?

Story

Though Coe doesn't speak with words yet, his repertoire of sounds is expanding, showing us that he understands that different sounds stand for different things. He is beginning to combine imitation with his own creative expression. For instance, seeing Jeanne take his picture, he reached for the camera and held it up to his face. Then, with a kind of whirring sound, he tipped his head back and began to tap the back of the camera with his hand. He is showing us he knows several things about cameras, including the pressing of a button and the sounds they make.

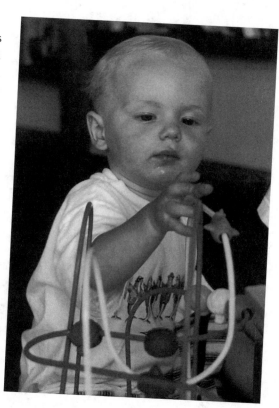

Coe has been increasingly interested in the bead rack. Today as he played with it beside Jeanne, he took her hand and placed it carefully on a few beads. As she moved a bead along the track Jeanne made a brrrruuum-motorlike sound. Coe looked from the bead to Jeanne's face as if to confirm the source of the sound. Before long, he too made a brrruuum-motor sound as he pushed the beads.

We are so impressed with Coe's communication skills and hope that as he learns actual words, his creativity in this arena won't go away. We wonder if he will transfer these sounds to other motions with similar materials and will test that out in the coming week. We will also be watching how attentive he is to other sounds and be introducing him to the tape recorder. It will be interesting to note other efforts he makes to engage us or his peers in his play.

Adding Visual Elements to Your Story

Along with your observation notes, other pieces of data will be useful to help you fill in the details of a story you want to make visible. Sketches, photos, audio- or videotape recordings, examples of things children have made, and resources you have offered all serve to help you understand and then translate your observations into a meaningful story.

Sketches

Taking a moment to sketch what children have made is a way to learn more about it, as well as offer a visual image in your storytelling. You don't need to be a great artist for this task. Simple sketching just helps you to see and represent the details. This is especially useful when you don't have a camera handy and you want to remember something children have built or created with materials like blocks, Lego plastic building blocks, buttons, and art or recyclable materials. When children see you sketching what has been made, they often want to do this too. This re-representation process can help their understandings shift and deepen.

Natalie's Blocks

A number of the children are experimenting with asymmetry. Natalie built this structure out of unit blocks. She added some blocks as I drew it to see if the structure would stay balanced.

Samples of Children's Work

Most early childhood programs typically send the children's work home with them each day. This gives the children the opportunity to show their creations to their families, and it keeps classrooms from becoming cluttered. As portfolio assessments have come into favor, teachers are saving more of children's work into some kind of filing system to be used for assessing, planning, and conferencing with parents.

Another benefit of saving samples of children's work, either in files on or display, is the opportunity to bring it back to them for further consideration. A child might revisit what she has done and decide to take it a step further. Or, she may be provoked to find more language to explain what was on her mind. Groups of children can look over each other's work and decide to collaborate on something similar together. All of these possibilities suggest that you may want to integrate children's work samples into your documentation.

Including actual examples of children's work in your observation stories is a great way to draw more attention to what you describe. When children really want to take something home, you may want to use a camera, scanner, or copy machine to keep a copy for your documentation. This option allows you to enlarge or reduce the size to fit into homemade books or visual displays.

Putting It All Together

After you have practiced the various approaches to writing described above, you will begin to identify which will work best for you and your situation. Whether you write alone, or collaboratively with teammates, you will begin to develop your own style and system to efficiently turn your observations into visible stories. Here's a summary of the important elements of any approach you use:

- Study your specific notes, transcripts, photos, and children's work samples. Identify the theme—what's the important story here? Choose one or more perspectives to write from—the child's story, the learning and development story, the teacher's story.
- Know the audience for your story—the children, their families, coworkers and other educators, the public and policy makers. This may influence your vocabulary and what you choose to emphasize.
- Write an introductory paragraph with simple text giving an overview of the context and theme. Start your writing by listing or webbing some lively words or phrases that capture the details you want to express. Then develop sentences. Try to avoid jargon.
- Choose the photos, work samples, and transcription of children's words that exemplify your story. If you want, you can include brief text with specific photos highlighting what you want the viewer to notice. For instance, if you are describing a child's efforts at writing and how that indicates what he already knows about literacy, under an accompanying photo you might say, "Juan carefully made his letters the same size by drawing a line for each of them to rest on."

- Write a final paragraph restating the meaning of this story in another way. Consider including a quote or excerpt from some professional literature or sentences highlighting another perspective on the story—the child's or your thinking process as a teacher.

Creating Displays and Homemade Books

Displays and books allow you to share the story of your observations visually, along with photos, artwork, transcriptions, and other details of the children's work.

Poster-Size Displays

The point of creating a visual display of your story is to give it attention and respect. While you may want to add your own creative elements, be sure these don't detract from, but rather help keep the focus on the children. It is their lives, words, and thoughts that you are trying to make visible. It may help you to look over the book *Spreading the News: Sharing the Stories of Early Childhood Education,* for specific ideas on graphic design elements. The examples of display panels featured there show a wide range of sophistication in applying basic design principles. *Spreading the News* also describes a four-step process for designing display panels. Another useful resource book is *Teacher Materials for Documenting Young Children's Work: Using Windows on Learning,* which shows a variety of display strategies to accompany the related book, *Windows on Learning: Documenting Young Children's Work.*

As you assemble your material for display, here are some general guidelines to apply:

- Remember that less is more. Arrange photos and text in an uncluttered fashion so that the different parts don't compete for the attention of the viewer's eye.
- Choose photos that show a close relationship between the child and another child or an object in the picture. Enlarge your best photos.
- If using a computer, use the same typeface or font throughout. Write a header in large print and subheads in the next size down.
- Include samples of the work under discussion, either photo reductions or enlargements, or actual pieces of the material.
- If your display is fairly clean and simple, you can add another graphic element such as a large silhouette of something in your story as a background for your display.
- Add three-dimensional elements where possible by mounting photos on foam core or cardboard before posting them to a display. You can also create a small shelf for children's work by folding cardboard or foam core board into a shelf that can be attached to your display.

Homemade Books

Some of your observations can be put directly into notebook binders or home-made books, while others can be transferred to books after they have been displayed on walls. Notebook binders with plastic sleeves are a simple solution for preserving documentation of extensive projects. Those with a plastic sleeve on the cover allow you to add a title page with some visual element.

Smaller stories that represent a sound bite about childhood lend themselves well to a simple homemade book. These immediately capture the attention of children and adult readers alike. Here are some simple directions for different kinds of homemade books and displays, gathered from a variety of sources.

Rubber-Band Books

- Choose as many pieces of scrap cardstock paper as you need for pages in your story.
- Stack your paper together, and fold each one to create a crease about 2 inches from the end.
- With the creased ends all together on the left side, create a hinge or decorative binding to fold over all the pages on the left end; glue down this hinge on the front and back sides.
- Punch two holes, evenly spaced, through the hinge or decorative binding and through all the papers.
- Use a long rubber band from the back side, threading each end through each of the holes.
- On the front side slip a small twig, chopstick, crayon, or marker through each end of the rubber band to hold it in place.
- Add your photos and text.

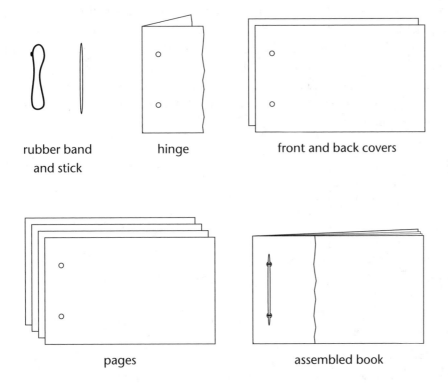

rubber band
and stick

hinge

front and back covers

pages

assembled book

Accordion Books
- Choose a stack of cardstock paper any size.
- Take one piece of paper and cut it into strips about 2 inches wide.
- Fold each of these strips in half, lengthwise, and use them as a hinge to glue two of your other sheets of paper together.
- Make as many of these two-page hinged sections as you need for your story, then attach them together accordion style with more hinges.
- Add your photos and text.

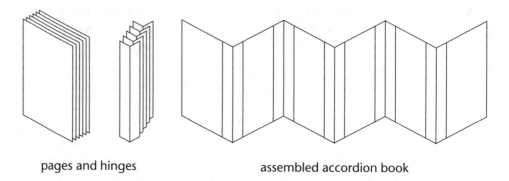

pages and hinges   assembled accordion book

Triaramas
Create a triarama for short, simple stories of children's activities. Turn a piece of thick paper, or even an old file folder, into a three-dimensional triangle with a photo and brief description of something a child has done.

- If your paper isn't square, begin by folding the right corner down to the lower left edge to form a triangle. Crease the long edge. Cut off the excess paper on the end.
- Open and fold the opposite corner down, creating another crease so as to have four quadrants when you open the paper.
- Cut from any one corner along the fold, stopping at the center of paper.
- Slip one of the cut sides on top of the others and glue to form a Triarama.
- Add your photo and text.

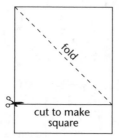 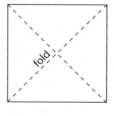 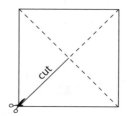 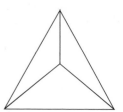

cut to make square

Binder Books

Take your observation notes, transcripts from children's conversations, photos, and reduced photocopies of children's work and put them into a simple notebook binder with plastic sleeves. This is especially effective for documenting longer-term group projects or ongoing portfolio entries or stories of individual children.

- Highlight elements of your story with some consistent-colored paper as background for your writing and data samples.
- Experiment with reducing or enlarging the size of the children's words or work you include.
- Be consistent with a design element that shares the story of your thinking and meaning-making process.
- Make an attractive cover and put the book in an accessible place for the children, their families, and program visitors.

The last pages of this book offer examples of a variety of these homemade books and visual displays. You can refer to these again and again, along with the resources listed, for examples and inspirations of organizing your observation data to make children's lives visible.

Make Your Vision for Childhood Visible

As you become a more observant, aware teacher, your teaching practice will transform. You will find more satisfying relationships with the children and their families, and your curriculum and learning outcomes will be more significant and authentic. Developing the art of mindfulness tends to bring more pleasure and liveliness to your overall life. You'll start noticing all kinds of details that keep your senses active and your heart humming. This inspires others who begin to sit up and take notice. Who is this lively person and what makes her or him so enjoyable and interesting to be around? As a result of your influence, others will begin to see children as a source of enrichment for their lives. They will see you as a model for the kind of life they'd like to be living. In effect, you become a leader, someone who is able to help others discover new potential in themselves.

Assuming leadership is a natural result of developing the art and skill of awareness as you bring your vision for childhood alive. Once you are on the road, casting a light ahead, others will want to join in and help shape the path. Think back to the poem in two voices that started this book. The tug-of-war teachers find in themselves can be diffused by becoming a careful listener, observer, and narrator. The stories we gather and make visible can reassure parents and supervisors and make teaching a more satisfying and compelling profession. Joining our voices two by two, we can become a persuasive chorus, bringing our communities more in tune with the value of childhood.

Recommended Resources

Carter, M., and D. Curtis. *Spreading the News. Sharing the Stories of Early Childhood Education.* St Paul: Redleaf Press, 1996. This book has many colorful examples of documentation displays, how to create them, and how to use them for a variety of purposes.

Diehn, G. *Making Books That Fly, Fold, Wrap, Hide, Pop Up, Twist and Turn.* Asheville, North Carolina: Lark Books, 1998. Because this book was created for children, the designs and instructions are not only easy to understand, but their forms capture the playful spirit of an early childhood program.

Helm, J., S. Beneke, and K. Steinheimer. *Windows on Learning. Documenting Young Children's Work.* New York: Teachers College Press, 1998. This book offers a systematic and comprehensive approach to documentation and assessment in children's programs.

———. *Teacher Materials for Documenting Young Children's Work. Using Windows on Learning.* New York: Teachers College Press, 1998. The work sheets and illustrations of this book are a quick reference for those wanting to implement some of the strategies suggested in the *Windows on Learning* text.

MacDonald, S. *The Portfolio and Its Use. Book II: A Road Map for Assessment.* Little Rock, Arkansas: Southern Early Childhood Association, 1996. The layout and format of this book make it easy to understand and put to use. It includes helpful charts describing what children learn in different areas of preschool environments.

———. *The Portfolio and Its Use. Developmentally Appropriate Assessment of Young Children.* Little Rock, Arkansas: Southern Association on Children Under Six, 1992. This book offers valuable examples of assessing the developmental stages represented in a child's work sample.

Richards, C. *Making Books and Journals.* Asheville, North Carolina: Lark Books, 1999. If you want to make professional-looking journals and books for your classroom, the author offers you clear instructions and illustrations to follow.

Sample Documentation
Displays

As you develop your observation skills and discover how extraordinary the every day moments with children are, you will find yourself motivated to invent attractive ways to make this visible to others. This can be done on bulletin boards and display panels, or in homemade books and frames as described in the previous chapter. Filling your program with visual displays of children's activities sends the message that they are worthy of recognition. Children will refer to these visual stories often and use them as a launching pad for further activities. Using these same formats to make the children's families visible in your program gives them the recognition they, too, deserve and develops a sense of belonging to a community. Watching this process unfold alerts you to the deeper significance of your work.

Each of the following pages offers an example of how providers and teachers have created beautiful, engaging formats to share their observation stories. These books and displays represent not only an effective communication strategy for our visually oriented, fast paced culture. They are also treasured, enduring gifts for the children and their families. Your visual stories help all of us see and value the vibrant, important time of life called childhood.

This section includes photos and text from four documentation display panels, two triaramas, an accordion book, a rubber band book, and a binder book.

Rachael Wants to Write

Rachael watched with a furrowed brow as her caregiver, Kara, wrote her daily reports on the couch. Rachael stood on her tiptoes to peer closely as Kara wrote. When Rachael pointed to the reports, Kara asked, "Would you like to do some writing too?" Rachael nodded and smiled. Kara handed Rachael a small clipboard and pen. Rachael grasped the pen in her right fist. She made wide, sweeping squiggles on the top page. She stopped and peeked at what Kara was doing. She then flipped to a clean page on the clipboard and continued writing. A loud noise distracted her, and she dropped the pen and walked away to investigate the sound.

Rachael's Learning and Development

Rachael imitates adult actions. Rachael has begun to understand that written language is meaningful. Rachael is realizing how writing tools work.

Teacher's Story

Now that we know that Rachael is interested in adult imitation, what next? We will continue to provide Rachael with lots of real items to enhance her dramatic play.

Miranda & Brittney Are Friends

Today Miranda and Brittney filled buckets with sand and carried them to the red wagon.

They each had an idea about where to put the buckets. They told each other their ideas and figured out how to fit the buckets in the wagon together.

They brought more and more buckets until no more would fit in the wagon.

But they each wanted to put in another yellow bucket. They figured out how to do it. How did they make them all fit in the wagon?

Now how many buckets are in the red wagon?
Another friend came along. Tyler wanted to fit his full red bucket in. Miranda and Brittney tried to make it fit.

They turned the wagon around, with Miranda pulling and Brittney pushing. These two girls started running faster and faster.

Round and round they went. One time all around, then two times. They were going really fast but they watched and were careful not to crash into any of the other kids also going around fast.

They went around again. But uh-oh, look what happened! The wagon wheel slipped into the sand. Miranda and Brittney lifted the wagon, but Manuel was coming around the curve really fast and he couldn't stop. There was a little crash, but no problem. They called for help, and teacher Cindy came to the rescue.
What do you think they did then?

Building Connections

Ryan D. was playing at the playdough table all by himself. He was building a house for the mama and baby turtles. Ryan J. asked him, "Can I play with your turtles?" Ryan D. responded, "My turtles are all taking a nap right now, so you can't come in. But you can build your own house over there."

Ryan J. took up the suggestion and built his own round house for the frog family. As they worked on their own, they talked about each of their family homes. "Mine has a bedroom and a living room." New connections began to unfold as Ryan J. offered, "Look, I'm making a backyard to your turtle house. Is that okay?"

"Sure," Ryan D. agreed. They decided to work together to build a central area with a beautiful rock fence around it. As their houses began to connect, their friendship grew.

Fast Friends

Tyler, Manuel, Francisco, and Jerry went right to the bikes today the minute we got outside. This is something they almost always do. After riding around the circle two or three times, making whirling, speeding sounds, they all went to the fence and one by one, without talking about it, got off and lined their bikes up.

They got right back on again with Jerry taking the lead. Round and round they went going faster and louder with each lap. Suddenly Jerry's bike tipped over and he fell forward.

"Stop! Stop!" called Tyler, getting off his bike and going to help Jerry. Manuel and Francisco jumped off their bikes and hurried over. Tyler leaned down and began to lift Jerry up by the arm. "Get him! Get him! Help! Help! Help me get him!" Jerry pushed himself up the rest of the way and the boys all headed back to their bikes and the fun began all over again.

Sometimes when children race their bikes, take risks, and make loud sounds, we have the urge to stop them. We worry that they might get hurt or we may not like all the loud voices. But if we stand nearby to keep them safe, we can watch closely and try to see what this must feel like for them.

Children find all sorts of ways to explore what their bodies can do, how much power they have, and how to make friends with other children. It often looks different from what adults would like to see, but it helps them grow in their confidence and skills.

Grandma Goodrich
and Neil

A family interview and a quick observation were made into triaramas.

Grandma Goodrich's Hopes and Dreams

My grandchildren are helpful and independent. They may be spoiled and may be experiencing some feelings of loss because of being away from their mother. My dream is for them to become responsible and caring members of society, to get a quality education including college and become whatever they want to be.

Neil Explores Spatial Relationships

Neil has recently become interested in fitting small things into larger things. He delights in putting small toys into baskets and taking them out again. He has a long attention span for such activities, often sitting for up to fifteen minutes repeating this action. Very recently, we have noticed Neil exploring these spatial relationships with his body. He finds cozy spots in which to fit his body. This is a challenging and developmentally appropriate activity for Neil.

A Crew of Rocket Ship Builders

This observation story was documented and made into an accordion book for the children to revisit their work.

Let's make the rocket ship really big. Is there enough room for all of us?

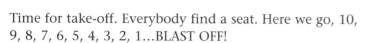

Time for take-off. Everybody find a seat. Here we go, 10, 9, 8, 7, 6, 5, 4, 3, 2, 1...BLAST OFF!

These tubes are the giant rocket boosters. We will blast off really far to outer space.

Who is driving the rocket ship? Keep us on course for outer space!

A House for the Fairies

This observation story was documented and made into a rubber-band book.

A House for the Fairies

A group of children were playing together in the sandbox this morning. They collected pinecones, dandelions, pine branches, and grass clippings to build a house for the fairies. Their discussion centered around how they could attract and catch a fairy.

Here's how they described their work.

"This is a track for races and gymnastics. I think they would like to live here with those."

"We have to make an arrow so they know which way to go to the house."

"Here's some clover for their food."

"They need a bench and a swing."

"I'll make them a soft bed. Then they will come and fall asleep and we can catch one."

"I know, let's put honey in here. They will like the sweet and it will get all over them and they will stick."

"Fairies are really real. I know we will catch one."

Ramp Studies

This binder book documents an ongoing interest in ramps in one preschool room.

Since the beginning of the preschool year, building ramps and roadways for cars in the block area has been a continuing interest for many of the children. Children play the game of racing, and they zoom the cars along tilted blocks over and over again.

Noticing this ongoing interest in ramps, the teachers begin to study the ideas and theories underlying the children's play. What do they seem to find so engaging about zooming cars? What are they exploring and learning about the world through this play? We offer new materials and document the children's activities for them to build upon. This will help us learn how to keep this study going.

As the children notice the cars flying off the sides of the ramps they begin to build walls out of blocks to keep them on the track. The teachers make sure we take pictures and share this strategy with the ramp-builder group.

The children use the photo documentation from a previous day's work to build this complex ramp. They have added the blocks on the top of the ramp to create a tunnel. The excitement surrounding this new ramp focuses on the cars as they disappear and then reappear.

Nicholas and Eric discover that they can tilt the table for another version of a ramp. They add blocks to create roadways for their Lego cars to race down. They are most interested in how fast they can get their cars to go, and in the way they crash and break into pieces at the end of the ramp.

Index

Notes:

i indicates an illustration.

This index is alphabetized letter-by-letter. Leading function words in subentries are not alphabetized.

A

Ackerman, Diane
A Natural History of the Senses, 42
Alerta: A Multicultural Bilingual Approach to Teaching Young Children (Williams and DeGaetano), 115
Alvarado, Cecelia, et al.
In Our Own Way, 115
An American Childhood (Dillard), xii
art of awareness activities
drawing
contour drawings, 92–93, 101
finder drawings, 44–45, 52
exploring
influences on your perceptions, 10–12
mirrors, 104–105
looking and seeing
looking closely (outdoors), 24
observing nature, 57
seeing up close (with a jeweler's loupe), 34–35
as study session component, 6
unmasking emotional responses, 66–67
word webs, 78–80, 146–147
Ashton-Warner, Sylvia
Teacher, 89
assessment checklists
math assessment, 122*i*
audiotapes
as tools for gathering documentation, 137

B

Bad Guys Don't Have Birthdays (Paley), 76
Beautiful Stuff (Topal and Gandini), 53
Before Push Comes to Shove (Levin and Carlsson-Paige), 101
Best Day of the Week (Levin and Carlsson-Paige), 101
The Block Book (Hirsch), 53
Boys and Girls (Paley), 76
The Boy Who Would Be a Helicopter (Paley), 90
Bringing Reggio Emilia Home (Cadwell), 89
Brosterman, Norman
Inventing Kindergarten, 52
Bruchac, Joseph
on the circle of life, 141

C

Cadwell, Louise
Bringing Reggio Emilia Home, 89
California Tomorrow
Looking in, Looking Out, 115
Carroll, Colleen
How Artists See Animals, 22
Carson, Rachel
on a child's sense of wonder, 60
The Sense of Wonder, 42, 60
on sensory exploration, 33
Carter, M. and D. Curtis
Spreading the News, 152, 156
Catching the Wind (Ryder), 63, 64
Chaffee, John
The Thinker's Way, 52
Chesterton, G. K.
on children's sense of the strange and humorous, 43
childhood
experiences, remembering (*See* remembering childhood experiences (activities))
images of, in children's literature, 30–31
making your vision visible, 155
as significant part of life cycle, 25
themes, in ordinary moments, 119
as time for strong family connections, 105–106
as time of building relationships, 94–95
as time to construct meaning, 80–81
as world of exhilarating and scary adventures, 67–69
as world of magic and discovery, 35–36
as world of natural wonders, 57–58
as world of possibilities, 45–47
Children at the Center (Pelo), xiv
City by Numbers (Johnson), 64
Clemens, Sydney Gurewitz
The Sun's Not Broken, A Cloud's Just in the Way, 89
computer hardware and software
comparison pricing on cnet.com, 138
Considering Children's Art (Engel), 89
Cortez, Jesus
Infant and Toddler Caregiving, 115
Creating Better Child Care Jobs (Center for the Child Care Work Force), 140
Curtis, D. and M. Carter
Reflecting Children's Lives, 129

D

Davidson, J. I.
    Emergent Literacy and Dramatic Play in Early Education, 89
Delpit, Lisa
    Other People's Children, 115
    on seeing through our beliefs, 9, 109
descriptions
    and interpretations, noting differences (activities), 13, 17–18
    photo captions vs. descriptive stories with photos, 146*i*
    practice describing details (activity), 16–17
    valuing ordinary moments, xiii, 118–119
    word webs, to generate descriptive details, 78–80, 146–147
    writing from three perspectives, 147–149, 148*i*, 149*i*
Desert Quartet (Williams), 64
Diary of a Baby (Stern), 31
Diehn, G.
    Making Books That Fly, Fold, Wrap, Hide, Pop Up, Twist and Turn, 156
Diffily, D. and K. Morrison
    Family Friendly Communications for Early Childhood Programs, 129
Dillard, Annie
    on children and learning, xii
documentation examples, 157–166
    accordion books, 164*i*
    binder books, 166*i*
    Building Connections, 161*i*
    A Crew of Rocket Ship Builders, 164*i*
    Fast Friends, 162*i*
    Grandma Goodrich and Neil, 163*i*
    A House for the Fairies, 165*i*
    Miranda & Brittney Are Friends, 160*i*
    poster-size displays, 159*i*, 160*i*, 161*i*, 162*i*
    Rachael Wants to Write, 159*i*
    Ramp Studies, 166*i*
    rubber-band books, 165*i*
    triaramas, 163*i*
Drummond, Tom
    representation for learning activity, 88–89

E

early childhood programs
    and generational apartheid, xii
ECENET-L (on-line discussion group), 123
ECEOL-L (on-line discussion group), 123
Elkind, David
    generational apartheid, xi–xii
Emergent Literacy and Dramatic Play in Early Education (Davidson), 89

Emotional Intelligence (Goleman), 76
The Emotional Life of the Toddler (Lieberman), 76
Engel, Brenda
    Considering Children's Art, 89
Everyday Mysteries (Wexler), 22
Exploring Writing and Play in the Early Years (Hall and Robinson), 90

F

Family Friendly Communications for Early Childhood Programs (Diffily and Morrison), 129
The Family of Children, 17
Felstiner, Sarah
    math assessment, 122
    on moments to capture, 131
    observation of ordinary moments, 118–119
    observation of Power Ranger play, 143
    using observations in planning curriculum, 121–122
Fialka, Janice
    It Matters, 115
First Feelings (Greenspan, S. and Greenspan, N.), 31
Forman, George
    on making children's ideas visible, xiv
Fuller, Buckminster
    on sensory exploration, 40

G

Gallas, Karen
    The Languages of Learning, xv, 89
    on pedagogy of creating the classroom as a research community, xv
    Sometimes I Can Be Anything, 75
    Talking Their Way into Science, 129
Gelb, Michael J.
    How to Think Like Leonardo DaVinci, 52
The Geography of Childhood (Nabhan and Trimble), 64
The Girl with the Brown Crayon (Paley), 129
Goleman, Daniel
    Emotional Intelligence, 76
Gonzalez-Mena, Janet, 109
    Multi-Cultural Issues in Child Care, 115
Gotta Minute? (Lawrence), 140
The Great Outdoors (Rivkin), 64
Greenman, Jim
    Places for Childhood, 31
Greenspan, Stanley I. and Nancy Thorndike Greenspan
    First Feelings, 31

H

Hall, Nigel and Anne Robinson
    Exploring Writing and Play in the Early Years, 90
Hannaford, Carla
    Smart Moves, 76

Hannigan
   Off to School, 115
Helm, J., S. Beneke, and K. Steinheimer
   *Teacher Materials for Documenting Young Children's
      Work,* 152, 156
   Windows on Learning, 152, 156
The High/Scope K-3 Curriculum (High/Scope
   Foundation), 132
Hirsch, E. S.
   The Block Book, 53
Hoffman, Donald
   on understanding what we're seeing, 5
   Visual Literacy: How We Create What We See, 5
How Artists See Animals (Carroll), 22
How to Be Organized in Spite of Yourself (Schlenger and
   Roesch), 140
How to Think Like Leonardo DaVinci (Gelb), 52
Hucko, Bruce
   A Rainbow at Night, 90
   Where There Is No Name for Art, 90
Hunger of Memory (Rodriguez), 115

I

Infant and Toddler Caregiving (Cortez), 115
In Our Own Way (Alvarado et al.), 115
*Intimate Landscapes: The Canyon Suite of Georgia
   O'Keeffe* (Self), 42
Inventing Kindergarten (Brosterman), 52
isometric perspective designs, 20*i*
I Spy (Scholastic Books), 21
I Spy Something (Leonard), 140
It Matters (Fialka), 115

J

Jablon, J., A. Dombro, and M. Dichtelmiller
   The Power of Observation, 140
Johnson, Stephen T.
   City by Numbers, 64
Jones, Elizabeth, xiv
Jones, Elizabeth and Gretchen Reynolds
   The Play's the Thing, 90

K

Keller, Helen
   on the sense of smell, 35–36
Kent, Corita
   on being aware of what we don't know yet, 55
   on children's perspective on the physical world, 23
   Learning by Heart, 44, 92
   on recovering the ability to see, 1
The Kindness of Children (Paley), 101
Kohl, Herb
   on children's stories, 77

L

Lamott, Anne
   on family pictures, 103
The Languages of Learning (Gallas), xv, 89
Lawrence, I.
   Gotta Minute?, 140
Learning by Heart (Kent), 44, 92
learning goals
   children connecting with the natural world, 56
   children exploring, inventing, and constructing, 43
   children forming relationships and negotiating
      conflict, 92
   children's eagerness toward representation and
      literacy, 77
   children seeking power, drama, and adventure, 65
   children's perspectives, 24
   children using their senses, 34
   children with their families, 104
   learning to see, 9
learning to see (study session), 9–22
Leaves of Grass (Whitman), 65
Leonard, A.
   I Spy Something, 140
Levin, Diane E.
   Remote Control Childhood, 76
Levin, Diane E. and Nancy Carlsson-Paige
   Best Day of the Week, 101
   Before Push Comes to Shove, 101
Lieberman, Alicia F.
   The Emotional Life of the Toddler, 76
Lizard in the Sun (Ryder), 63, 64
Look: The Ultimate Spot-the-Difference Book
   (Wood, A.), 21
Looking in, Looking Out (California Tomorrow), 115

M

MacDonald, S.
   *The Portfolio and Its Use. Book II: A Road Map for
      Assessment,* 132, 156
   *The Portfolio and Its Use: Developmentally
      Appropriate Assessment of Young Children,* 156
Magic Eye: A New Way of Looking at the World, 21
Making Books and Journals (Richards), 156
*Making Books That Fly, Fold, Wrap, Hide, Pop Up, Twist
   and Turn* (Diehn), 156
Master Players (Reynolds and Jones), 90, 129
Metamorphosis: The Ultimate Spot-the-Difference Book
   (Wilks), 21
more things to do (activities)
   adult friendships, thinking about, 100
   artists' work, observing, 52
   bubbles, playing with, 41
   bubble solution recipe, 41
   contour drawings, 101
   current view of children, exploring, 30

"Dear Beautiful Butterfly" letter, 63
decoding symbolic representations, 88
emotional responses, studying, 75
finder drawings, 52
"how we did it," sharing memories, 114
images of childhood in children's literature, exploring, 30–31
isometric perspective designs, 20i
jeweler's loupes, 42
Magic Eye 3-D designs, 21
no two things are the same, discovering, 63
optical illusions, 18i, 19i
other forms of representation, 88
relationships, remembering difficult moments, 100–101
representation for learning, 88–89
risk taking, assess your response, 74–75
shifting perspectives, reflecting on, 21
spot the difference/find the details, 21
standing in another's shoes, 114
as study session component, 7
try another perspective "just for a day," 63
using your nose, 42
Much More than the ABC's (Schickedanz), 86
Multi-Cultural Issues in Child Care (Gonzalez-Mena), 115
Murphy, Pat and William Neill
By Nature's Design, 64

N

Nabhan, Gary Paul and Stephen Trimble
The Geography of Childhood, 64
A Natural History of the Senses (Ackerman), 42
Nature Hide and Seek: Jungles (Wood, J.), 22
Nature Hide and Seek: Oceans (Wood, J.), 22
By Nature's Design (Murphy and Neill), 64
Nimmo, John, xiv

O

observation
for detail, 15
differing views and conflict, 12
as guide for teacher's plans and actions, 3, 120–122
inspiring good teaching, 1
invitation to take a closer look, xii
keen observers, becoming, xvi–xvii
and mental filters, 12, 17
open-ended observation, 3
observation of children (study sessions)
components of study sessions, 4–7
connecting with the natural world, 55–64

eagerness toward representation and literacy, 77–90
exploring, inventing, and constructing, 43–53
forming relationships and negotiating conflict, 91–101
learning to see, 9–22
perspectives, 23–31
seeking power, drama, and adventure, 65–76
with their families, 103–115
using their senses, 33–42
observation practice (activities)
Bad Guys on the Playground (story), 69–71
A Balancing Act (story), 72
Bubble Symphony (story), 37–38
creating parking lots, for initial responses, 13–14
Dancing with Shadows (story), 26–27
First Frost (story), 59–60
A Furry Friend (story), 60–61
A Game about Good-bye (story), 107–108
A Glitter Path (story), 39
I Want My Dolly Back! (story), 97–99
Look What I Understand (story), 84–86
Lost Dog (story), 83–84
Making Things Right (story), 27–28
Movin' to Marco (story), 95–96
My Life As a Dog (story), 28–29
noticing descriptions and interpretations, 13
Potty Time (story), 109
practice describing details, 16–17
putting it all together, 17–18
recognizing components of observation skills, 14–16
Stay Out of the Sand (story), 108–109
as study session component, 6–7
Take Me Out to the Ball Game (story), 108
Toddlers and Tubes (story), 49
Under the Cedar Tree (story), 47–48
We Can Get Along (story), 97
observations, documenting
documentation examples (*See* documentation examples)
enhancing disposition, knowledge, and planning, 118–122
enhancing partnerships with coworkers and families, 126–127
as guide for teacher's plans and actions, 120–122
irritating behavior, researching, 119–120
metaphor of beads on a string, 134
record keeping (*See* record keeping)
sharing, with coworkers and children's families, 120
stimulating children's learning, 124–125
valuing ordinary moments, 118–119
observations, making visible. *See* telling stories

Off to School (Hannigan), 115
O'Keeffe, Georgia
    on seeing flowers, 91
Olds, Anita
    on children as miracles, xii
on-line discussion groups, 123
optical illusions, 18*i*, 19*i*
ordinary moments, valuing, xiii, 118–119
organizing to make childhood valued, 131–140
    methods to suit your style, 132–134
    notes on children's actions and conversations, 133*i*
    other tools for gathering documentation, 137–140
    simple and short observations, 134–135
    work environment considerations, 135–137
Other People's Children (Delpit), 115
Outside Lies Magic (Stilgoe), 64
overview of study sessions, 1–8

P

Paley, Vivian Gussin
    Bad Guys Don't Have Birthdays, 76
    on boredom, xv–xvi
    Boys and Girls, 76
    The Boy Who Would Be a Helicopter, 90
    The Girl with the Brown Crayon, 129
    The Kindness of Children, 101
    Wally's Stories, 129
    You Can't Say You Can't Play, 101
pedagogy of listening, observing, and documenting,
    xiii–xvi
Pelo, A. and F. Davidson
    That's Not Fair!, xiv–xv, 129
Pelo, Ann
    Children at the Center, xiv
    on evolving pedagogy of listening, observing, and
        documenting, xiv–xv
    on making observations visible, 142
    Setting Sail, xiv
    on sharing observations to stimulate learning,
        124–125
    on sharing observations with families, 127
    Thinking Big, xiv
    work environment considerations, suggestions,
        136–137
perceptions, influences on
    exploring and understanding, 10–12
    mental filters (activity), 17
photographs
    captions vs. descriptive stories with photos, 146*i*
    as tools for gathering documentation, 137–140
Places for Childhood (Greenman), 31
The Play's the Thing (Jones and Reynolds), 90

*The Portfolio and Its Use. Book II: A Road Map for
    Assessment* (MacDonald), 132, 156
*The Portfolio and Its Use: Developmentally Appropriate
    Assessment of Young Children* (MacDonald), 156
The Power of Observation (Jablon, Dombro, and
    Dichtelmiller), 140
Prescott, Elizabeth
    metaphor of observations as beads on a string, 134
The Private Eye: Looking/Thinking by Analogy (Ruef),
    34, 42

Q

quotes about seeing
    being aware of what we don't know yet, 55
    a child and play-acting, 65
    children's perspective on the physical world, 23
    children's sense of the strange and humorous, 43
    children's stories, 77
    a child's sense of wonder, 60
    the circle of life, 141
    family pictures, 103
    kids doing nothing, 57
    moments to capture, 131
    noticing clouds, 44
    observing small wonders, 24
    recovering our ability to see, 1
    reflect on shifting perspectives, 21
    seeing flowers, 91
    seeing through our beliefs, 9, 109
    sense of smell, 35–36
    sensory exploration, 33, 40
    as study session component, 5
    teaching and guiding discovery, 29
    understanding what we're seeing, 5
    using observations about children, 117

R

A Rainbow at Night (Hucko), 90
record keeping
    audiotapes, photographs, and videotapes, 137–140
    documentation examples (*See* documentation
        examples)
    math assessment, 122*i*
    metaphor of beads on a string, 134
    methods, adopting to suit your style, 132–134
    notes on children's actions and conversations, 133*i*
    research questions, 124*i*
Reflecting Children's Lives (Curtis and Carter), 129
reflecting on quotes
    being aware of what we don't know yet, 56
    children and play-acting, 66

children's perspective on the physical world, 24
children's stories, 78
family pictures, 104
seeing flowers, 91
seeing through our beliefs, 10
sensory exploration, 34, 40
teaching and guiding discovery, 29
refocusing teachers' work, xi–xiii
Reggio Emilia schools, xiv
REGGIO-L (on-line discussion group), 123
remembering childhood experiences (activities)
childhood conflicts, 95
connections to childhood, affirming, 106
drama and adventure, 69
favorite memories, 25–26
important relationships, 94–95
loose parts, exploring and inventing with, 46–47
reawakening your senses, 36
as study session component, 6
the wonders of nature, 58
your own storytelling, 81
Remote Control Childhood (Levin), 76
research question records, 124*i*
Reynolds, Gretchen, xiv
Reynolds, Gretchen and Elizabeth Jones
Master Players, 90, 129
on using observations about children, 117
Richards, C.
Making Books and Journals, 156
Rico, Gabriele Lusser
Writing the Natural Way, 78, 90
Rivkin, Mary S.
The Great Outdoors: Restoring Children's Right to Play Outside, 64
Rodriguez, Richard
Hunger of Memory, 115
Ruef, Kerry
The Private Eye: Looking/Thinking by Analogy, 34, 42
Ryder, Joanne
Catching the Wind, 63, 64
Lizard in the Sun, 63, 64

S

sample observations
Experimenting with the Ramp, 51
Exploring Danger and Safety, 82
Grace Makes Art with Nature, 62
Hot Lava, 68
I Superman, 67
math assessment, 122
as notes for curriculum plans, 121–122
ordinary moments, 118–119
Rhonda's classroom, 1–2
Rocket Blasters, 48

Rock Power, 73
writing from three perspectives, 149
Schickedanz, Judith
Much More than the ABC's, 86
Schlenger, S. and R. Roesch
How to Be Organized in Spite of Yourself, 140
school-age programs
and generational apartheid, xii
Self, Dana
Intimate Landscapes: The Canyon Suite of Georgia O'Keeffe, 42
self-reflection, promoting, 117
The Sense of Wonder (Carson), 42, 60
Setting Sail (Pelo), xiv
Smart Moves (Hannaford), 76
Smith, Robert Paul
on kids doing nothing, 57
Sometimes I Can Be Anything (Gallas), 75
Spreading the News (Carter and Curtis), 152, 156
Staley, Lynn
on teaching and guiding discovery, 29
Stern, Daniel
Diary of a Baby, 31
Stilgoe, John R.
Outside Lies Magic, 64
stories worth telling, 142–145
study sessions
components, 4–7
how to use, 7
overview, 1–8
reasons for use, 3–4
users' comments about, 4
The Sun's Not Broken, A Cloud's Just in the Way (Clemens), 89

T

take another look (activities)
annoyances, turning into research questions, 123
artwork, explaining, 123
audio or video for immediate review, 126
children's work, studying, 87
child's perspective, taking, 30
conflicts and problem solving, 100
descriptive sensory words, 41
family books, 111, 112*i*, 113*i*
family discussion pages, 128
family interests, customs, and rituals, 110–111
family members, sharing stories of their childhoods, 111
found materials, using, 51
how children think about their families, 110
in-depth curriculum themes, 124
the language of friendship, 99–100
literacy in your environment, supporting, 86

literacy play, 86
mental filters and influences on perception, 17
observation book to send home, 128
observation of children
    with animals or other living creatures, 61
    finding playmates, 99
    in natural settings, 61
    negotiating risk, 73
    play involving power and adventure, 73
    at work, sketching, 126
observation practice, putting it all together, 17–18
observations, sharing via computer, 128
open-ended materials, 50–51
other representational materials in your
    environment, 86–87
parent notice board, 127
self-directed skills, 123
self-portraits and name writing, studying, 87–88
sensory exploration, 40–41
sequencing cards, 126
staff observation sharing system, 128
as study session component, 7
theme books, 126
Talking Their Way into Science (Gallas), 129
TAWL (on-line discussion group), 123
Teacher (Ashton-Warner), 89
Teacher Materials for Documenting Young Children's
    Work (Helm, Beneke, and Steinheimer), 152, 156
teaching
    and observation, 1
    organizational suggestions, single or team
        teachers, 136
    refocusing work, xi–xiii
telling stories, 141–156
    accordion books, 154, 164*i*
    to become history books, 145
    binder books, 155, 166*i*
    with children's work samples, 151
    for coworkers and children's families, 143–145
    documentation examples (*See* documentation
        examples)
    to give back to children, 142–143
    important elements, putting it all together,
        151–152
    make your vision for childhood visible, 155
    photo captions vs. descriptive stories with
        photos, 146*i*
    poster-size displays, 152, 159*i*, 160*i*, 161*i*, 162*i*
    rubber-band books, 153, 165*i*
    sketches, adding, 150, 150*i*
    triaramas, 163*i*
    word webs, to generate descriptive details, 78–80,
        146–147
    writing from three perspectives, 147–149, 148*i*, 149*i*

That's Not Fair! (Pelo and Davidson), xiv–xv, 129
The Thinker's Way (Chaffee), 52
Thinking Big (Pelo), xiv
Topal, Cathy Weisman and Lella Gandini
    Beautiful Stuff, 53

U
using observations about children, 117–129
using the book, xvii

V
videotapes
    as tools for gathering documentation, 137–140
visual elements and telling stories, 150*i*, 150–151
Visual Literacy: How We Create What We See
    (Hoffman), 5

W
Wally's Stories (Paley), 129
web sites
    cnet.com (www.cnet.com), 138
    Magic Eye (www.magiceye.com), 21
Wexler, Jerome
    Everyday Mysteries, 22
Where There Is No Name for Art (Hucko), 90
Whitman, Walt
    on child and play-acting, 65
    Leaves of Grass, 65
Wilks, Mike
    Metamorphosis: The Ultimate Spot-the-Difference
        Book, 21
Williams, Leslie and Yvonne DeGaetano
    Alerta: A Multicultural Bilingual Approach to
        Teaching Young Children, 115
Williams, Terry Tempest
    Desert Quartet, 64
    Windows on Learning (Helm, Beneke, and
        Steinheimer), 152, 156
Wood, A. J.
    Look: The Ultimate Spot-the-Difference Book, 21
Wood, John Norris
    Nature Hide and Seek: Jungles, 22
    Nature Hide and Seek: Oceans, 22
writing
    from three perspectives, 147–149, 148*i*, 149*i*
    as a way to find and tell stories, 145–150
Writing the Natural Way (Rico), 78, 90

Y
You Can't Say You Can't Play (Paley), 101